YOU ARE MEANT FOR MEANT FOR GREAT THINGS

MY STORY OF TURNING SETBACKS INTO STEPPING STONES

MARCIA DONZIGER

BookBaby Publishing

COPYRIGHT © 2023 MARCIA DONZIGER

YOU ARE MEANT FOR GREAT THINGS
My Story of Turning Setbacks into Stepping Stones
Learn more at www.MarciaDonziger.com.

To order in bulk or inquire about a speaking engagement, contact Marcia@MarciaDonziger.com.

Paperbook ISBN 978-1-66786-852-3

Ebook ISBN 978-1-66786-853-0

United States

For Jake and Ryan, the true *miracles* in my life.

In loving memory of Uncle Chad Amos Wheeler,
whom we lost too soon.

Table of Contents

PREFACE

December 10, 1991. I was twenty-two years old when an eighteen-wheeler Mack truck slammed into my car during morning rush hour. I was driving to San Diego State University for my final senior year exam before graduation. It was taking four-and-a-half years to graduate since I added a business management minor degree to my organizational psychology major late in the game. Given the significance of the day, I dressed in an emerald green silk blouse and my favorite black jeans, an outfit that gave me an extra jolt of confidence. I had almost—*almost*—reached my goal of college graduation. My well-laid plan was to go into human resources.

I merged from southbound 5 to eastbound 8, a maneuver I had done hundreds of times before. But that morning as I curved along the on-ramp in the right lane, a semi-truck was fast approaching on my left. He didn't see my little blue Nissan Sentra and drifted into my lane. Pushing down hard on the horn, I screamed "STOPPPPP!" but to no avail. His massive truck hit my tiny car at full speed. I crashed into the cement wall and ricocheted back into traffic, spinning out several times. The slow-motion 360-degree view of the freeway, the cement walls, and the passing cars blurred.

I heard crunching metal as my car crashed into the median. Charcoal gray plumes spiraled out the hood darkening the light blue sky. Multiple cars swerved and skidded to a screeching halt, nearly hitting each other. The truck driver managed to stop his semi and ran to pull me out of the wrecked car. He called 911 and laid me out on the asphalt in the middle of the freeway. Scared for my life, wailing sirens became louder and more intense as an ambulance arrived and loaded me onto a gurney.

My best friend and roommate Tami met me at Scripps Mercy Hospital ER downtown. The car was totaled, yet against all odds, I escaped relatively unscathed with only a case of whiplash and a sore back. Talk about lucky fortune, divine intervention, or both.

Out of the blue, Tami whispered, *"You were meant for great things."* She may have said this because it was my third accident in a year. I had survived two others in which the cars had also been totaled, including being hit by a drunk driver. But by some miracle, I kept walking out alive, indicating (to her at least) that there had to be some higher plan for my survival.

Tami's words planted a seed. A seed so deep that I have thought about these words each time I have faced obstacles in my life. And believe me, my life has been full of obstacles.

Five years after that car accident, I was diagnosed with Stage 3 ovarian cancer. I survived the cancer, but the permanence of infertility was a devastating blow at the age of twenty-seven. Infertility sent me on a long road to achieve my lifelong dream of becoming a mom. I also went through two divorces and made several career pivots. I started a cancer nonprofit organization that almost failed and then led the rebuild, resulting in a merger with one of the nation's most well-respected cancer organizations. Stress caught up with me a few years ago, when I suffered agonizing back pain and underwent major surgery.

With all these hard experiences, I've learned a thing or two about resilience. Getting knocked down in life is a given. It's how we get back up that matters most.

Life lessons can be excruciatingly painful but also invaluable: for me, they generated a life I love, one that is fulfilling beyond my wildest dreams.

This is my story of forging forward when life hands you the unthinkable. What I know is that each of us has the power to create and choose our path, no matter who or what sideswipes us along the way. I was meant for great things. And so are you.

PART I:

WAKING UP TO A
NEW REALITY

1

LIFE SPINS OUT OF CONTROL

"You will never change the fact that being human is hard, so you must change your idea that it was ever supposed to be easy."

—GLENNON DOYLE, UNTAMED

Out of the deepest slumber, I am jolted awake in a sterile, cold room. Pinned to the bed, the relentless sensation of knives stabbing through my stomach and back cause me to thrash around in pain.

Dr. Kamel, my gynecologist, is standing over me. The beeping machines remind me that I am in Northwestern Memorial Hospital in Chicago. I have had abdominal surgery to remove an ovarian tumor. But Dr. Kamel's troubled expression causes panic to flood through my body. Something isn't right.

"Marcia, I'm so sorry," Dr. Kamel says softly. "The tumor wasn't benign after all." She pauses uncomfortably. "You have cancer. We took everything out. You've had a complete hysterectomy."

My ears hear the word cancer, but my mind fixates on never being able to have children. It doesn't help that Dr. Kamel is six-months pregnant and delivers the devastating diagnosis while my eyes are level with her swelling pregnant belly.

I squeeze my eyes shut and black out. Hours later, in the middle of the night, I wake up sweating in darkness and hit the morphine button. I am allowed to hit it every six minutes, and at 5:59 each interval, I press that button as if my life depends on it.

My mind races. I try to understand, what happened? The surgery was *supposed* to have been a simple procedure. Dr. Kamel felt sure the tumor was benign, and that at worst I'd maybe lose one ovary. The recovery was expected to be quick, and I'd be back to work in a week. I should be returning to my Chicago apartment, my job as a flight attendant, and my busy life with Ed, my husband. I'd gone off birth control five months earlier because we were planning to start our family.

In an instant, everything had changed.

The cramps and bloating I'd felt for months had not been harmless. They were signs of ovarian cancer silently spreading through every organ in my abdomen. The day after my surgery, a team of gynecological oncology doctors came into my hospital room to share more information.

My formal diagnosis: Stage IIIc ovarian cancer.

How was this possible? I was twenty-seven years old. I'd never heard of anyone my age with ovarian cancer.

In my mind, I replayed the conversation with Dr. Kamel ten days earlier in her office.

"Marcia, it turns out there *is* a reason you were having symptoms," she said. "We've found a tumor in your ovary."

"Could it be cancer?" I asked, immediately filled with fear.

"No—you're too young to have cancer," she said decisively. I was shaken but relieved. Her tone implied that the tumor was inconvenient but not life-threatening.

Well . . . sometimes even doctors are wrong.

• • •

Taking morphine was as much for my mental anguish as my physical pain. In my mind, I had fallen into a thousand-foot well with no ladder leading to stable ground.

Gone were my lifelong dreams of having children. Gone, too, was any certainty about my life moving forward. My work as a flight attendant for American Airlines. My eighteen-month marriage. Our plans to move to the Southwest U.S. My entire future, or so it seemed.

After the hysterectomy, the doctors prescribed six months of chemotherapy, since the cancer had spread into my lymph nodes. It was a terrifying time of endless doctor appointments, days of nonstop nausea, depression, anxiety and insomnia, and persistent feelings of FOMO (fear of missing out). The one thing I was spared was losing my hair. I was grateful for this small miracle, but that also led to the disorienting feeling of *looking* completely normal on the outside while feeling irreparably damaged on the inside.

In a way, my physical challenges, while daunting, were not as difficult as the emotional ones. At a time when my friends were traveling, partying, dating, marrying, and settling down, I was confronting my own fragility and mortality. I felt completely alone despite the incredible support of my loved ones.

• • •

Strangely, I didn't feel relief after my treatment was over. It was nerve-wracking *not* having appointments to go to. *Were the doctors doing everything possible to prevent a recurrence? So now what? Did the treatment work? Would the cancer come back again?*

I'm a doer. And I wanted to fight cancer with everything I had. I had gotten through my treatment by putting one foot in front of the other, trusting in the protocol my medical team advised. Now that I had reached the finish line with nothing further to do, I felt at a loss.

There was now a clear division in my life—BC (Before Cancer) and AC (After Cancer). It would take a while to realize that without having experienced cancer firsthand, I might not have undertaken many of the challenges I took on in the following years. In the most surprising ways, cancer forged who I am today and revealed my strengths. Like learning to live with vulnerability and adapting to unforeseen changes. Maintaining optimism in the face of uncertainty. And moving forward even when I might not feel like it. Perhaps most importantly, during the worst of times, I learned to focus on what I had to be grateful for.

I was acutely aware that I lived in a city where I could receive high-quality treatment from a team of talented doctors. I had great health insurance, which many people are not fortunate to have. I was also thankful for how incredibly supportive most of the people in my life were. My parents, sister, friends. My husb—wait.

This is where you insert the sound of a needle scratching a record. If you had told me my marriage would go down the drain while I was undergoing cancer treatment and grieving the loss of my fertility, I might have laughed at the absurdity of it all. But that's exactly what happened. And now, with time and perspective, I see the gifts (and in retrospect, some good humor) wrapped in traumatic experiences, despite the pain.

2

WHEN YOUR ROCK TURNS OUT TO BE A PEBBLE

"The saddest part about betrayal is it never comes from your enemies."

—UNKNOWN

The veneer of self-sufficiency is ripped away when you get a life-threatening illness. In the weeks and months following my diagnosis, I felt like a tree in winter, stripped bare, with all my vulnerability on display.

I was now firmly in the AC part of my journey, where I had space to reflect on what the experience had taught me. Cancer reveals many things. One thing it taught me was how much I hated to ask for help. Cancer also showed me who was there for me. Sadly, one of the people I thought would be my biggest supporter turned out to be a dud.

I learned that Dr. Kamel came to the waiting room to tell my husband, Ed, and my mom that they had discovered I had ovarian cancer.

The news was, of course, shattering to them, but to my mother's surprise, Ed broke down. Full-on panic attack. I later learned he was taken to the Crisis Intervention Center; I'm sure the hospital staff there thought *he* was the one who had just received the dire diagnosis.

I know what you're thinking. *Not* a good sign. I tried to rationalize Ed's reaction. I reminded myself that my cancer diagnosis terrified him and meant infertility for us as a couple, not just for me. But the truth was, I needed to believe that we would get through this *together*.

Unfortunately, Ed's self-centered behavior only intensified throughout my treatment process. How was it that the man who was supposed to be my rock, the person I could rely on through thick and thin, through sickness and health, was instead showing himself to be a pebble?

My mom, who had been a constant source of support for me throughout my life, became the rock for both of us on D-Day (aka "Diagnosis Day") and in the weeks that followed. My dad also flew to Chicago from my hometown of Anaheim, California, as soon as he heard the news. That first week I was in the hospital, my loving parents were the ones who hugged me, smoothed my hair, and reassured me that everything was going to be all right. Meanwhile, my husband became, in effect, a second patient. He embraced his new victimhood with gusto, telling friends how much he was struggling.

I don't really blame Ed for being devastated. It's just that his distress was all-consuming. He was upset over having a sick wife, and yet I was the one having toxic chemicals pumped into my bloodstream and suffering from fatigue, nausea, insomnia, anxiety, and depression. The metal taste in my mouth lingered for days. The only thing that removed the horrible taste was white peppermint Tic-Tacs (which I cannot eat to this day because they remind me so vividly of that period of my life).

I quickly learned about the compounding effects of cancer. Immediately following my hysterectomy, I experienced surgically induced menopause, with intense hot flashes and night sweats. The surgery also caused an extremely painful bowel obstruction that sent me back to the hospital for another week.

Cancer is like a Category 5 hurricane that rips through life and leaves in its wake pain, grief, and loss. Loss of my female reproductive organs, loss of my sense of immortality, loss of my ability to have children, and a general disintegration of the future I'd just started building with my husband.

Thankfully, I was eligible for short-term disability through American Airlines. I was home for the first four months of treatment and had just two more months to finish my chemo regimen when Ed, much to my bewilderment, pushed me to return to work.

In retrospect, I wished I'd listened to my intuition that I needed more time to heal. Meanwhile, American Airlines grounded me in a flight operations role at the airport, which allowed me to work even though I couldn't fly due to my compromised immune system. In a cruel twist of fate, all the other grounded flight attendants were pregnant and about to go on maternity leave. So, while I was in the office mourning the loss of my fertility, my peers bonded over impending motherhood. One day it all became too much. I secluded myself in the supply closet, along with the paper towels, rubber gloves, and industrial-sized cleaning bottles, and sobbed for two hours.

But that was nothing compared with the day my parents had to return home to Anaheim. Holding them tight, tears streaming down my face, I knew Ed could never give me the warm, loving care that I craved.

This truth made me ache all over. It was clear that my husband— the man who had promised to have and to hold me until death do us part—was incapable of fulfilling his vows. In fact, every day, he was pulling farther and farther away from me.

Ed continually told me how I needed to ease *his* burden. He expected me to do more housework and shamed me when I couldn't live up to his stringent expectations. He wanted the energetic career woman I had been before cancer struck. Before my sixth and final chemo treatment, I proposed we get a puppy to boost our spirits and bring some joy back to our lives. I hoped a puppy—having something of our own to care for—would unite us. Ed didn't like the idea, but I begged him, and he finally said yes. So, we adopted a little black-and-white mutt and named her Angie. She was adorable yet a lot to manage. Between chemo and full-time work, I had little energy to spare. Angie needed to be let out around 4:00 a.m. daily, and wouldn't you know that Ed refused to help? "That's YOUR dog," he'd say coldly. After three long weeks, I just couldn't cope anymore.

"Can we find her a better home?" I asked. That's when he cruelly dropped another bomb. "No, why don't *you* leave? I'm attached to the puppy." *Yes, you read that right.*

Ed raised the idea of my leaving again when I mused about the possibility of our moving from Chicago to the West Coast or the Southwest. Maybe a change in environment would restore our relationship, especially since we agreed to move before my diagnosis. "YOU move back to California. I'm never leaving Chicago," he barked.

Why was my husband repeatedly telling me to move across the country without him? How could he not know I was thinking wishfully about our future, not seriously planning to leave my doctors in the middle of treatment? And why was he talking as if I were a single unit?

There was no "we" anymore. Maybe there never had been.

I now clearly understood that Ed was ill-equipped to handle my illness and the effects of infertility. Things came to a head one Saturday a few months into my chemo treatment.

My close friend, Sara, called from Orange County to share the news that she was pregnant. The sun was streaming in through our living room window as Ed sat nearby, listening to our conversation. I was genuinely overjoyed for Sara. She and I had been on the same life track for many years, graduating from college at the same time, starting our careers, getting married, and now, for one of us, having a baby. I managed to keep it together while on the phone but burst into tears as soon as I hung up. Sara's dream of having children was coming true, while mine would never happen.

Instead of comforting me, Ed hissed, "Stop crying! Control yourself! Stress causes cancer!"

I looked at Ed and realized how far we'd grown apart. Honestly, I no longer recognized him. After months of him telling me to move back to California alone, I asked him a simple question.

"Am I that replaceable?" Maybe I was feeling masochistic, or maybe I just needed that last dose of clarity. Ed looked at me with eyes devoid of empathy. "Yes, Marcia. We're all replaceable." And the final nail went into the coffin.

I finally got the hint. Like I said, the guy was a pebble.

• • •

December 31, 1997. The end of a year from hell. The cancer treatment ended, and I had been served divorce papers just after Thanksgiving. On New Year's Eve (yes, I love the symbolism), my sister, Meryl, flew to Chicago to help pack my life and move back home to Anaheim with my parents. She supported me during this fraught time as I packed clothes, books, and photographs into boxes. It was astonishing how quickly a life could be dismantled.

A week earlier, Ed had left for a solo three-week vacation that was scheduled, I am sure, to avoid any messy emotional exchanges.

Before walking out of our bedroom for the last time, I left our wedding album open on our bed. I wanted it to be one of the first things he saw when he came home to an empty house. I knew he would relish playing the victim, as he always did, but we both knew the truth: he had driven me away.

Everything felt surreal. The home we had built together was not mine anymore. And the marriage I thought would last forever had collapsed.

When at last the Chicago cab arrived at the home I was leaving, Meryl turned to me. "Are you ready?" she asked tenderly. In tears, I nodded. She hugged me and reassured me that I was not alone and that everything would be OK. I was amazed at how the tables had turned. Meryl is my younger sister, and for all our lives, I felt the need to take care of her. Now, I was the one who needed help, and she was consoling me. It was a full-circle moment.

We flew out of O'Hare Airport on January 1, 1998. With my sister squeezing my hand, I gazed out the window, in shock over how fast life had turned upside down. The clouds passed by in a haze. My grandma Ellie always said nothing lasts forever, even the devastation of heartbreak. Trying to summon her spirit and calm my nerves, I repeated "this too shall pass" to myself throughout the entire plane ride.

My parents welcomed me with open arms as I walked back into my childhood home in Anaheim where my emotional healing could begin.

• • •

I flew back to Chicago three months later to finalize my divorce. Ironically, it was also the one-year anniversary of my cancer diagnosis (the cancer community calls this a "cancer-versary"). I was nervous to see Ed again, but he never bothered to show up. So typical that he didn't even come to say goodbye after all we'd been through. Alone, I signed the divorce papers he'd served me just three months earlier. We never spoke again.

Some things are a mystery. I'll never know if Ed decided he didn't want me because I couldn't bear his children, because my illness spooked him, or because he couldn't bear the thought of a cancer recurrence. Or maybe it was something deeper, something that had nothing to do with the circumstances we found ourselves in. Perhaps he simply wasn't mature enough to accept the cards life had handed us.

Looking back, I feel grateful that I learned about Ed's character before children tied us together for the rest of our lives. Sometimes it takes a crisis like a cancer diagnosis for people to really show you who they are.

Nineteen ninety-seven was the worst year of my life, yet it paved the way to my best life. The trifecta of events in that one-year period—ovarian cancer, infertility, and divorce—completely changed my life's trajectory. It also showed me the power of community and the love and support which surrounded me.

I have amazing parents, a sister, and grandparents who instilled in me lessons of resilience to keep moving forward. I wouldn't have made it through this horrible period without them. That year also taught me the importance of having good, dependable friends. You don't need a lot of them, but you need the bring-you-chicken-soup-when-you're-sick kind of friends. I discovered I had those, too, in abundance.

I'll never forget my dear childhood friend Annie, who flew from California to sit with me in the hospital every day after my hysterectomy. During chemo, a different friend came with me to each session, including Tami, my college roommate, who flew in from San Diego. My flight attendant friends Cindy, Lisa, and Kim cooked healthy meals and played scrabble with me, a welcome distraction.

My experience with cancer (and with Ed) taught me to take regular inventory of the people in my life. It's an important lesson. Are the people who surround you rocks you can depend upon, or have a few pebbles snuck in there? You know the types—the ones who are great talkers but aren't reliable. The ones who come to the dinner party empty-handed. The ones who ask for a lot of favors and take far more than they give. Those who don't show empathy when you need it most.

Life is too short to spend with people who don't appreciate you and who are unable to give back, particularly during hard times. Cancer revealed with startling clarity that I only want to spend time with people who are kind, generous, and compassionate. You'll recognize these people when you meet them because they make your spirit soar. When you leave after having spent time with them, you feel seen, valued, and accepted for who you are, despite your scars.

As my healing began, I knew in the deepest part of me that I would be OK.

3

THE DEATH OF EXPECTATIONS

"Some of us think holding on makes us strong, but sometimes it is letting go."

—HERMANN HESSE

After my marriage crashed and burned, I felt disoriented and unsure how to put the pieces of life back together again. Living at home with my parents in Anaheim, my bedroom was like a 1980s-time capsule from my teen years. Rob Lowe posters hanging onto my walls with old, yellowed scotch tape. Yearbooks piled high on the bookshelf containing proof of embarrassing haircuts. Fringed leather jackets and blazers with huge shoulder pads hanging lifeless in the closet. My pink rotary phone—the one I spent hours on with my friends dissecting every move of the boys we had crushes on—still sitting on my nightstand. Even the off-white, plastic mini-blinds were the same ones I'd gazed through as a moody teenager. *How was it that I felt like I'd aged a hundred years but could so easily slip back into my sixteen-year-old self?*

I often lay in my bed and heard my mom and dad talking in the kitchen. While their voices comforted me, the reality hit me hard. This was *not* where I pictured myself living again at twenty-eight years old.

I had built a life and career in Chicago. My marriage failed hard, and it was depressing to think of starting over again. While I was now surrounded by loving family, rather than my narcissistic ex-husband, inside, I was mourning the loss of how I thought my life would be. I needed time to adjust to my new normal.

Many of us reckon with the death of expectations in our relationships. Someone you trust with your whole heart who betrays you. Friends who make choices that are detrimental to their well-being. The picture-perfect marriage that turns out to be not-so-perfect. Here's the reality: you can't control anyone but yourself. I've learned that acceptance is a key ingredient to moving beyond our current circumstances. Disappointment is a part of life, so the sooner we give ourselves (and others) grace, we can start to forgive those who have hurt us. And the sooner we do this, the sooner we can forge a new path forward with a lighter heart.

As Brené Brown writes in her book *Rising Strong*, "If we care enough and dare enough, we will experience disappointment. But in those moments when disappointment is washing over us, and we're desperately trying to get our heads and hearts around what is or is not going to be, the death of our expectations can be painful beyond measure."

The death of my expectations *was* painful. And grieving them was a prolonged process. I was forced to think anew, top to bottom.

While I never imagined being divorced, I needed to accept this as my reality. I'd mostly seen success stories. My parents are still together after fifty-four years. My grandparents had a fifty-year love story before my grandfather passed away. Even Ed's parents had been married for decades.

Young as I was, I also couldn't assume good health. Before my diagnosis, I exercised, ate well (even trying to get five servings of vegetables a day), and got enough sleep (mostly). And I still got cancer.

Then there was the dream of having children. I assumed I'd give birth to my own children. Why wouldn't I? I couldn't wait to see what physical characteristics they would inherit. My grandma's irresistible smile? My father's mustache and sense of humor? Mom's warmth and patience? I couldn't wait to caress my swelling belly, to feel the miracle of a baby kick inside me. I even looked forward to morning sickness.

The scariest thing of all was letting go of my expectations for a long, healthy life. Before cancer, I never thought twice about mortality. I had plenty of time to figure things out, and in this way, I took the days and years for granted. Now, every day felt precious, since my future was not guaranteed. Faced with my mortality, it was up to me to decide how to make the rest of my life mean something.

I was never one to rush headlong into anything without a plan—that's simply not me, as any of my friends would be sure to tell you. But if I truly wanted to change my life, I knew I had to set goals and pursue them with all my heart and every ounce of energy I had.

Everyone hopes for a long life, yet at some point, we're forced to see that time is finite. While this is an uncomfortable truth, it's incredibly valuable because it gives us a sense of urgency. During my cancer experience, a friend gave me a gratitude journal. At first, I scoffed. *What did I have to be grateful for…cancer, infertility, a failed marriage?* I learned that whenever I focused on good things, my mood and outlook improved tremendously. I wrote about waking up for another day, the strength to take a walk, healthy food on my plate, the endless love from friends and family. There was so much to be grateful for.

Below are some of the affirmations which helped me through this time and which I continue to rely on today:

- Learn to accept what you cannot control—which is most things.

- Strive to be happy instead of right.

- Fill your life with friends and colleagues who share your values—kindness, respect, generosity, loyalty.

- Build a career that gives you an opportunity to leave the world a better place.

- Search for the good in any situation and appreciate what's working.

Becoming conscious of my own mortality turned out to be an unexpected blessing. I couldn't snap my fingers and turn back time. But I could move forward with a fresh perspective and a new beginning.

In the end, I can say that the loss of my marriage, my health, and, yes, my expectations for the future led me down a path of radical reinvention.

PART II:

COMING TO TERMS

DARING TO DREAM AGAIN: REDISCOVERING MYSELF

"Life is too short to wake up in the morning with regrets."

—UNKNOWN

Officially divorced, I'd been living with my parents for five months now. I was starting to come to terms with my new life. American Airlines let me transfer to Los Angeles/LAX Airport so that I could keep my flight attendant job, my only lifeline to pre-cancer normalcy (and health insurance).

That spring, one of my girlfriends, Kim, a fellow flight attendant, suggested that we take a trip to Spain for a week. At first, I hesitated, still not feeling like my adventurous old self yet. "Come on, a change of scenery will do you good. It's time to start living again, Marcia!"

A trip to Europe with four of my girlfriends sounded tempting. I'd been depressed and licking my wounds, choosing to spend Saturday nights enjoying game nights with the "old folks" and my parents' friends whom I'd known all my life. I hadn't been ready to socialize or date yet. Maybe this trip was the catalyst I needed.

"You're right," I told Kim with a budding spark of hope. "*Vamos España!*"

Soon after, on a hot day in late May, I squeezed into a middle seat in coach, settling in for an uncomfortable all-nighter American Airlines flight from Los Angeles to Madrid. Watching the flight attendants give safety instructions, I marveled at how much I had changed and grown. Being out on my own again, single, and free. I felt alone yet liberated. Adventure awaited, my future a blank slate. Part of this reality excited me. *Anything can happen* was a faint whisper from my soul as I dozed off to sleep.

Twelve hours later, the door slid open at the jet bridge. Stepping off the plane, I opened my eyes and inhaled deeply. Even the air smelled different. My friends and I exchanged excited glances.

A crowded train took us into the center of town, and we arrived at the Novotel hotel. After freshening up, we went out to explore Madrid's narrow, cobblestoned streets. As if dehydrated from world culture, I drank in the sights and sounds of a foreign city, something that always invigorates me. The old, dark buildings with their elegant iron terraces crammed with potted plants; the small outdoor café tables; the curved glass street lanterns; the charming street signs. It was a far cry from Anaheim, and with each step, I felt part of my spirit coming alive again.

We heard loud cheers coming from a pub down the street. To our surprise, the Europa League Final football tournament was on full blast. The bars were packed with Real Madrid fans. Seduced by the celebratory sounds and thirsty from the crushing humidity, we entered the pub and ordered cold cervezas. The floors and tables were slick with spilled beer, and the pub reeked like a frat house. The jubilant mood was infectious. It didn't hurt, of course, that we were surrounded by dark, handsome men, all speaking (screaming) in Spanish, "GOOOOAAALLLL!" when their team scored.

You can imagine how a group of young, blonde American women (I was the only brunette) stuck out in a pub full of raucous, football-loving Spanish men. The fact that we were the only ones not watching the game on the television screens made us even more conspicuous.

The stars must have been aligned that night. Madrid won the game, and the city erupted into a bacchanalian frenzy. Delirious fans ran wild in the streets, overturning dumpsters, and chanting victory songs until early morning. It was like Pamplona's famous running of the bulls, only this night it was the running of the loco football fans.

As fans outside went crazy, the crowd inside our little pub thinned out. And that's when we heard two American men speaking English.

Our groups were immediately drawn to each other. George was the first to introduce himself. Soon his friend reached out with a strong, tanned arm to shake my hand.

I couldn't help noticing his blue eyes and devilish smile. "Hi, my name is Danny. What's yours?"

"I'm Marcia. Nice to meet you." His eyes widened with surprise when I told him I'd recently moved from Chicago to California.

"Small world!" he grinned. He was from Chicago, too.

Unlike George, who had dark eyes and dark hair (the type of man I'm usually attracted to), Danny was blonde with a slim build. Yet there was something magnetic about him. When he stepped closer to me, I felt a distinct shiver up my spine.

Danny, I learned, was a twenty-five-year-old medical student, originally from Detroit, attending the University of Chicago medical school. Ironically, he lived down the street from my old apartment. He was also a Chicago Cubs fan and loved the city with the same passion

I did. As our conversation continued through the night, everyone else seemed to recede into the background.

Danny was the first man I'd been attracted to since my marriage ended. I hadn't felt this kind of chemistry in years. Believing I was damaged and broken, I had totally forgotten myself as a woman who might be desirable. Meeting Danny reminded me that despite how shattered I felt inside, from the outside, no one could guess the ordeal I had gone through.

As we talked, I was struck by how intently Danny listened. For the first time in ages, I felt seen and beautiful.

Like a scene from a rom-com movie, Danny and I were insepa-rable for the next three days. My friends were understanding, knowing how much I needed to heal from the previous year's traumatic events. Danny and I decided to take a day trip to Toledo, a medieval town an hour from Madrid. We boarded a rickety tour bus and made our way to the back row. Danny sat next to the dusty window, and I lay down with my head on his lap.

Something about him inspired trust; I felt safe enough to confide in him about my cancer, the infertility, and my divorce. I don't know why I chose to share such intimate details with someone I barely knew. My instincts turned out to be right. As I opened up, Danny rubbed my head tenderly and listened. It was more than therapeutic. His deep capacity for empathy helped me see myself as worthy of affec-tion and love.

Danny and I spent a romantic day exploring the historic, walled city of Toledo, famed for its Arab, Jewish, and Christian monuments. We toured ancient castles and ate tapas in tiny cafés. We both felt that we had traveled back in time. I think I fell in love that day with Danny, with Toledo, and with the reawakened "me"—not a sick divor-cee defined by her illness and failures, but a healthy young woman deserving of a hopeful future.

When it was time to part, I wasn't prepared for how much I would miss Danny. He and George left Madrid to travel north to San Sebastian, while my friends and I continued our journey south to Sevilla. Hugging tightly, we didn't want to let go. Danny and I pledged to see each other in the United States. Part of me couldn't wait for the Spain trip to end so that I could see him again.

Luckily, with my flight benefits at American Airlines, it was easy to visit Danny in Chicago. We began a passionate, long-distance love affair. It worked for nine months, but ultimately the relationship ran its course. Neither of us was willing to move. And besides, he mentioned something about a nurse named Gina.

I was heartbroken at the time yet also grateful. Danny came into my life at a critical juncture. With him, I learned to see past the horror of my cancer. He helped me transform into a confident woman who was able to trust men again. That trip to Spain reignited my belief that a happy future could be possible.

5

A BOLD NEW DIRECTION

"Edit your life frequently and ruthlessly.
It's your masterpiece, after all."

—NATHAN W. MORRIS

Sue, a friend from Chicago, had recently moved to Manhattan Beach, California, about an hour's drive from where I was still living with my parents in Anaheim. Sue is one of those beautiful, smart, funny all-American girls from Ohio. A girl you could be jealous of because she makes life appear easy. Once you meet her, you'd realize her success is due to her work ethic. Plus, she has zero ego. You'd fall in love with how effortlessly cool she is and want to join her posse.

One evening, I drove from inland Anaheim to visit her on the coast in Manhattan Beach. Sue's apartment was just steps from the Pacific Ocean. I was in awe. Noticing a book on her coffee table called *The Starter Marriage* (she, too, had recently gotten divorced), I immediately knew she was a kindred spirit. We were at the same stage in life, going through a similar rebuilding of our lives.

As a native Californian, the beach has always been my happy place. Right outside Sue's door, I longingly touched the warm sand, soaked in the calming waves, and inhaled the salt air.

Back in her apartment, Sue opened a bottle of cold chardonnay and poured two glasses. We sat on the couch, petting her sweet golden retriever, Austin, making easy conversation. Sue was looking for a roommate. "What do you think about living with me and Austin?" she asked.

I jumped up without hesitation, "Yes, yes, yes!" We hugged and talked about all the fun we would have together. This new opportunity laid down a stepping stone in my emotional healing process. I was ready to venture out again post-cancer, post-divorce and start to write my next chapter.

The beach apartment on Ocean Drive was just eight minutes from Los Angeles International Airport, my home base with American Airlines. Sue quickly became one of my favorite people and introduced me to a fun group of new friends. Our growing closeness, the comforting ocean air, and my newfound freedom revived me.

• • •

I was inspired by Sue's boundless energy, work ethic, and corporate career. By now I was twenty-nine and had worked for American Airlines for seven years. While I loved my travel adventures, the grueling, road warrior lifestyle was taking its toll. I had always known that working as a flight attendant would be temporary while I was young, not my lifelong career. Now that I was living on my own terms again, the time felt right to reset and carve a new path.

At this point in time, 1999, the technology industry was booming. Everyone was talking about the dot-com revolution, and I wanted to be a part of it. I was fascinated by the power of the Internet and, of course, enticed by the possibility of a higher-paying job.

My friend Janie worked for a computer distributor called Ingram Micro (IM). She was making significantly more money than me and having way more fun. Sales were through the roof, and IM was hiring. Janie introduced me to her manager, and I went to interview. The office was full of energetic young professionals, and it seemed like an exciting place to work. But I was extremely nervous due to the fact I had no sales experience. To make a long story short, I flunked the interview and didn't get the job.

On my way out of the office, however, I noticed a trade magazine in the lobby. *What if Ingram Micro had competitors I could approach for work?* I wondered.

Flipping through the magazine, I discovered that Ingram's biggest competitor was Merisel, headquartered in Los Angeles, literally five minutes from my house. This was too good to be true.

Then doubt set in. I hadn't gotten the Ingram Micro job. *What would make me think I'd get one at Merisel? Why would they hire me?* Pushing past my fears, I took a deep breath and called. The operator picked up, and I asked if they were hiring. The receptionist said, "Actually, we are!" She patched me over to a hiring manager named Sarah. I dropped off my application the next day.

A week later, I was invited for an interview. Sarah quickly perused my very short resume as I wrung my hands beneath her desk. She looked to be around my age. Finally, she looked up and beamed. "My mom is a flight attendant, too!" It was all smooth sailing from there. We connected over the fact that friends and family members of airline employees fly for free, and other airline perks. After about twenty minutes, Sarah said, "I think you can learn this. Would you like an entry job as a sales representative? There will be a very intense six-week training. We pay $50,000 to start."

$50,000?! I couldn't believe my ears. The starting salary alone was way beyond what I had been making after seven years with American Airlines. I jumped up and said "yes!" on the spot. The new job at Merisel not only connected me to my new passion—technology—but provided me with hands-on training. Forget the free passes. Now I could afford to buy my own airline tickets!

I'll be honest; the transition from flight attendant to office desk worker was tough. I missed the flexible travel perks, including the eleven days off a month, and the excitement of waking up in a new city every day. At Merisel, I was locked into a rigid schedule; I sat in my small cubicle, beginning at 7:00 a.m. and stayed there for nine hours each day. I was overwhelmed learning the intricacies of the thousands of hardware and software systems we sold.

I hung in there and kept pushing myself to learn as quickly as I could. Finally, about two months after I'd started at Merisel, things began to click. I knew I was going to make it when I figured out who to approach for help when I didn't know the answer to something.

Merisel was a vibrant and fast-moving business culture, full of twenty-somethings who worked hard and played hard. As the tech boom continued, sales literally fell into our laps. It was a rare opportunity to be in the middle of the action at a time of unprecedented growth. And there were other advantages too—no more jet lag, no more tasteless airline meals, no more missing out on fun evenings and weekends with family and friends. Most importantly, I felt proud of myself for pushing out of my comfort zone.

After a year at Merisel, a rare outside regional sales manager position opened. I wanted this job as there was potential for a huge pay increase. So, I tracked down the hiring director, Tom, and shared my interest. He quickly brushed me aside. "No, you don't have enough experience." Fair enough. Maybe he was right.

Still, Tom's immediate "rejection" ignited a fire inside. I decided not to give up and devised a strategy to change Tom's mind. I needed a "sponsor" above Tom's rank in the company to recommend me as a solid candidate. Without support, Tom would not give me a second look.

Thank goodness I had the foresight to find a mentor early on. He was Bill Page, who happened to be the president of Merisel.

Bill was one of those leaders you never forget. He was wise and generous with his time and expertise. Bill made a point of going to each employee's cubicle regularly to ask how we were doing; he had an open-door policy. Bill was the first leader I'd worked for who taught me what it took to lead a great culture. He respected and appreciated each employee no matter their rank. I saw firsthand how the staff looked up to him and how his kindness created a positive work culture. Bill's generosity spurred me to ask him early on if he could mentor me. We established monthly meetings where I would ask questions about the industry. Bill never made me feel stupid; he appreciated my curiosity and ambition.

At our next mentoring meeting, I asked if he thought I could do the sales manager job. Rather than tell me what to do, Bill coached me and gave me space to ponder the opportunity aloud with him.

I decided to be bold. "Bill, will you do me a favor and ask Tom to give me an opportunity to interview? That's all I ask."

"Absolutely." He started dialing the phone before I was out the door. An hour later, guess who called me to schedule an interview? Tom. He seemed to be more open-minded after getting a call from his boss. Funny how that works!

After a series of interviews with Tom and other colleagues, I was awarded the promotion. The new position had six-figure income potential, and I was able to double my income the next year. Even better, I was proud to earn the annual "Master Sales Award" for work ethic and sales results.

Much of this success was due to my marketing counterpart, Dyonne Woolen, who joined me on every sales call. We joked that we were the "dynamic duo" and challenged ourselves to win over the unhappiest customers by delivering exceptional service. Dyonne embodied the irresistible combination of charm plus competence. We spent so much time on the road that we even wrote a book interweaving our unique experiences as minorities in this country—hers as a Black woman, and mine as a Jewish woman. This manuscript may come to life someday, who knows? It's never too late.

One of the lessons I gleaned from this work experience is that we can reframe "no" into a stepping stone to "yes." Staying open to opportunities—even if I didn't feel 100 percent ready—helped hone my skills. Most importantly, I learned that if I wanted people to take a chance on me, I had to stand up boldly, raise my hand, and take a chance on myself.

6

FORGING FORWARD

"Living alone makes it hard to find someone to blame."

—MASON COOLEY

By age thirty-one, I had enough distance from my divorce and the cancer to gain strength and confidence. My new career path and success helped immensely. It's amazing how, when you achieve in one part of your life, it sometimes spills over into others.

I finally had enough money to live for the first time on my own, which was a major milestone. I moved to El Segundo, California (the more industrial, affordable beach town neighboring both LAX airport and Manhattan Beach) into a two-bedroom apartment. The neighborhood was dilapidated (I think there might have been a crack house across the street), but the space was great and allowed me to use the extra bedroom as an office. There was even a balcony off the living room (it overlooked the crack house, but I didn't care). I took pride in filling my apartment with new furnishings and accessories—silverware, a coffee pot, bookshelves, a white couch, marble coffee table, duvet cover, and crisp sheets. I decorated every room with framed posters from Italy, Chicago, and Greece, an ode to my love of travel. I also surrounded myself with knick-knacks and souvenirs from my trips with American Airlines. Part of the reason I could afford this large apartment was that many people didn't want to hear the airplane noise overhead. But for me, it was perfect. It sounded like freedom.

I had come far from when I was a flight attendant living with six roommates in a tiny two-bedroom apartment eight years earlier. Back then, we didn't even have our own bed. It was a pinch-me moment.

Now that I was truly independent, I set my sights on finding a new life partner. After years of dating post-divorce, I knew the qualities that mattered. If I saw any signs of hypochondria in a man I was dating, I'd remember Ed and run the other way. Ditto if I didn't have a good gut instinct. One thing I knew—I wasn't going to settle for someone who didn't see me as an *equal* partner. I became pickier with men, zeroing in on my goal to find and fall in love with a man I could trust. I was looking for a husband and father, and my standards were high.

I had been seeing a therapist to help me rebuild my sense of self-worth and overcome deep feelings of being "damaged goods." Cancer, after all, is a lasting adversary of positive self-esteem. Therapy also allowed me to reflect on why I had chosen someone like Ed in the first place. Initially, I thought his being a hypochondriac was an adorable quirk. At our wedding, a friend even toasted him, "When you call Ed and get his voicemail, you hear, 'Press 1 to hear the symptoms of the day. Press 2 to hear the symptoms of yesterday. And press 3 to hear the symptoms of tomorrow.'" After cancer, I realized too late that his "quirk" bordered on pathological.

Therapy also taught me which red flags to pay attention to. Armed with new knowledge and awareness that my future husband was not going to be delivered by FedEx, I committed to putting myself out in the world. I went out with friends to concerts and the beach, said yes to men who asked me out, and kept an open mind about new experiences. I also traveled a lot, to Italy, England, France, Costa Rica, and even Japan. It was a huge shift in my mindset.

Should you believe this was all one long, great party, it wasn't by a longshot. There were many times I felt depressed and hopeless, especially after bad dates with shallow men. Dating was like wandering through a desert being parched for connection. Most people in their twenties hadn't endured life-and-death challenges, so my story was one that most of my peers couldn't relate to. Even my grandma said to me, "You went through more in that year than I've been through in my entire life." She said it in a way that made it clear how much she admired my strength, but I still felt sadness about the difficult losses and failures.

Despite the highs and lows of dating post-cancer, I was determined and didn't want to waste time. My attitude was the one thing I could control in this process, and I knew I wouldn't meet my future partner by sitting at home, even in an apartment I loved.

PART III:

FAMILY MATTERS

7

AN OASIS IN THE DESERT

"You'll never be able to escape from your heart.
So, it's better to listen to what it has to say."

—PAULO COELHO

One weekend in February 2001, my cousin Andrea convinced me to fly to Phoenix with her to attend a weekend conference for Jewish singles. I was raised in a conservative Jewish family and knew I wanted to marry a Jewish guy, so what did I have to lose? I was losing hope in the men of L.A. anyway.

The first evening was a cocktail party at the Marriott in downtown Phoenix. At least 300 young professionals milled around a large banquet room with glittering chandeliers, a stage, and a dance floor. People were laughing and schmoozing as if they'd known each other all their lives. Andrea and I waited in line at the bar behind two handsome men. One turned around and put out his hand to introduce himself, and as we chatted, I noticed how good-looking the other man was. He was tall with chestnut-brown hair and kind blue eyes.

We ended up finding a table where the four of us could sit and chat more. I learned they were both from Denver. Adam, the talkative one, eventually peeled off to join other friends, and Andrea soon found an excuse to leave, too. There was an awkward moment of silence, but then Rob and I began to talk about travel and what we do for a living.

"I am in sales for a tech company and used to be a flight attendant," I said.

Intrigued, he asked, "Wow, what was that like?" I told him some of my war stories, like when one of my first-class passengers overindulged in vodka and threw up into a paper barf bag during the deplaning process after we landed. Rob laughed and confessed that he loved to travel too, reeling off a list of his favorite places.

From there, we were off and running. This mild-mannered man had a lot to say, I remember thinking. He also had an infectious smile. I wanted the chance to make him laugh.

"What do you do?" I asked. He told me about his cable equipment business that sold excess inventory to cable companies like Comcast. He'd started the company when he was twenty-four. I was impressed by Rob's ambition and intelligence and by how he had literally created something from nothing. But that wasn't all. It turned out we each had one sister who are both teachers, and we had grown up in similar Jewish backgrounds, which was hugely important to me.

As the evening wrapped up, Rob and I arranged to meet at the "Modern Kosher Eating" breakout session the following morning (even though neither of us kept kosher). We sat beside each other that Saturday and were equally bored by the conversation. Maybe fifteen minutes passed before Rob slyly whispered in my ear, "Do you want to bail and check out the African cultural festival next door?" I had noticed that morning that there was a flea market outside our hotel with booths selling African crafts, furniture, and jewelry. I was ready for some fresh air and immediately said yes.

As we perused the stalls, I picked up a carved ebony candlestick, and it slipped out of my hand, causing a loud crash. The flea market workers stared disapprovingly as I scrambled to put it back on the table. Rushing off with Rob, we giggled about my clumsiness.

After the weekend, Rob went home to Denver, and I flew back to L.A. I had no expectations that we would see each other again due to our busy work and travel schedules. Plus, the geographic distance was less than ideal. Two days later, a Fedex package was on my porch. Tearing into the box, I saw two beautiful, ebony candlesticks carved with elephants, my favorite animal. Inside was a note: "Try not to break these." I had a good laugh and was touched by Rob's gesture.

Over the next few months, Rob surprised me by calling randomly on his business trips from places like Brazil, Argentina, and the Philippines. Six months later, in August, he invited me to Las Vegas to celebrate my birthday. Rob assured me we would have separate hotel rooms, but this wasn't feeling like a casual friendship anymore.

Rob went all out, booking tickets for a Cirque de Soleil "O" show, a Venetian gondola ride, and a helicopter trip over the Hoover Dam. We played a little blackjack, ate delicious food, lounged at the pool, and took in the sights of the Strip, like the Eiffel Tower at Paris Las Vegas, the Bellagio water show, and Caesar's Palace. He was nice. He was normal. He was Jewish! He was also a complete gentleman, dropping me off at my hotel room door at the end of the night, never making me feel like I "owed" him anything. We connected on a level I hadn't expected.

When Rob and I went back to our respective cities, I missed him. I had not told him yet of my "damaged past"—the cancer, divorce, and infertility—since I had learned from previous dates made for awkward conversation. It's such a presumptuous, vulnerable thing to share. Imagine on date one or two, and one of you announces, "Hey! Thanks for dinner, and by the way, I can't have kids . . ." It's so awkward and a definite mood killer.

Rob was serious-minded, though, and I wanted to tell him sooner than later. So, the Monday evening after the Vegas trip, while we were on the phone, I worked up the courage to tell him, "I have something to tell you before we see each other again." I spilled the entire story. It was a lot to process, but Rob was compassionate. I'll never forget his response: "I can't say I'm not disappointed, but I'm still interested." I appreciated his honesty even as I wrestled with the familiar tinge of inadequacy, of not feeling like "enough" of a woman to bear children. Mostly, I appreciated Rob's genuineness. After what I'd been through, his sincerity and candor meant the world. As we continued dating, we discussed other options for becoming parents, like adoption or surrogacy. He agreed these were good options should we get to that point.

Soon Rob and I were talking every night and traveling regularly to see each other. Over these months, I learned that he was the kind of person who got an idea and turned it into reality. I also learned he had had similar dating struggles in his home state of Colorado, meeting flaky or superficial women. Like me, he had gone to the Jewish singles event because he was serious about finding a life partner. Meeting Rob felt like discovering an oasis in the middle of a desert.

A year after the Jewish singles conference, Rob and I got engaged. The proposal happened when I was visiting him in Denver one weekend. We had just come home from dinner, and I was in the bathroom getting ready for bed. When I opened the door, the bedroom was full of lit candles. Rob was holding a red ring box, which he opened, asking, "Will you marry me?" It was an unforgettable moment. His face glowed with expectation in the candlelight. My answer was a resounding "Yes!"

When I told my company that I was moving to Denver to get married, they created a new, expanded sales territory for me in Colorado and eleven surrounding states including Utah, New Mexico,

Kansas, Nebraska, Arizona, and more. I would be traveling by plane every week to a different state, which thrilled me.

Leaving my life and friends in California to start anew in Colorado was a big step. It was another leap of faith to live without family nearby again. I didn't know anyone in Denver, although I did really like Rob's friends, who warmly welcomed me and helped ease the transition.

We decided to have a destination wedding in the Rocky Mountains in Vail, Colorado. One hundred fifty friends and family flew in from all over the country and around the world on the weekend of June 29, 2003. My flight attendant friends flew in from Chicago, Boston, Seattle, Atlanta, Austin, Miami, and California. Even my former roommate, Sue, who was pregnant, flew in from India, where she now lived. Rob is an amazing party planner and paid for shuttles to transport our guests from their hotels to our wedding and rehearsal dinner venues.

Our cowboy-themed rehearsal dinner was held at Piney River Ranch near Beaver Creek. I wore a long, flowered dress with a red leather fringed belt, along with red cowboy boots, a blue cowboy hat, and a blue-jean jacket. Rob wore a black-and-white checkered flannel shirt, jeans, and a black belt with a silver buckle, along with a black cowboy hat and boots.

I'll never forget the bumpy, uphill, hourlong drive on shuttles to the ranch where we ate barbecue, danced to country music into the wee hours, and enjoyed panoramic views of the Rocky Mountains.

We were married that Sunday on a sunny mountain top in Beaver Creek, Colorado. Our guests even got to take a chairlift up the mountain. For a beach girl from Orange County, I literally had reached new heights. At 10,000+ feet elevation, our outdoor Jewish wedding ceremony was followed by an indoor reception with a fun band, dinner, and heartfelt toasts. I wore a long, form-fitting, beaded white bridal dress with spaghetti straps, and Rob was handsome in his black tuxedo.

To see my parents dancing with joy made me so happy. After everything they had helped me through, it felt like a momentous beginning for all of us.

The Monday after the wedding, Rob and I escaped to Nevis Island in the Caribbean for our honeymoon. We also explored the island of St. Martin and swam with the stingrays. I let myself anticipate a future full of love, romance, travel, and adventures—and yes, the possibility of raising children, somehow, someway.

• • •

After a relaxing honeymoon, we returned home and dove headlong back into our busy careers.

The early months of our marriage were smooth and comfortable. I was learning a lot from my new husband as he overcame obstacles in his business. Rob managed a growing employee base and every so often had the difficult job of letting people go. Shipments of inventory were often delayed, and at those times, Rob would be on the phone all night, finding ways around the never-ending obstacles.

I admired his diligence. He had a very calm temperament and never got rattled. He was intensely dedicated and an out-of-the-box thinker. I was raised to find a stable job with good benefits, but watching Rob build his own company made me think that maybe I could do that, too, one day. Little did I know yet, Rob planted a seed in me to flex my own entrepreneurial mindset in the future.

Rob was loyal and generous. When his best friend from college needed a bridge loan between selling and buying a new house, Rob gave it to him without hesitation, no interest charged. For our fortieth birthday year (we were six months apart in age), Rob treated us and three other couples to a trip to Cuba and Mexico.

We lived in a four-bedroom home that Rob owned before we met. The house was in Greenwood Village, a beautiful suburb south of Denver. Our master bedroom and home office were on the main level. The two upstairs bedrooms were separated by a Jack and Jill bathroom. The house was perfect for a family and even within walking distance to great elementary, middle, and high schools. To me, it was a dream home.

Rob had his eye, though, on a much larger house in Cherry Hills where we could raise the family we both wanted so badly. The house was more luxurious than anything I'd ever imagined. It even had a movie theater and swimming pool.

"No way. This is too much," I told him. What I also meant to say was, "How can we afford this?" Before our marriage, we had discussed finances to some extent, and I knew Rob's business was thriving. But I didn't know he was *this* successful.

I'd grown up in a modest ranch house in Anaheim. At 2,000 square feet, it was just right for a family of four, though nothing about it was over-the-top or luxurious. Rob was so confident in the future of his business that he convinced me it would be OK to purchase the Cherry Hills house. He assured me we could afford to pay mostly cash and take on a small mortgage.

Rob liked nice things but wasn't terribly materialistic. He didn't grow up affluent. He was self-made and worked hard for everything he had. While I also like nice things, having such a stunning house initially made me very uncomfortable. I realized on some level that I wasn't just wrestling with living in a mansion, but also with ambivalence about feeling that I deserved this kind of abundance.

The Cherry Hills house was move-in ready. I wanted to focus on starting a family, not furnishing a home, so this was a big plus. And despite the home's grandeur, I could easily envision raising kids there. The room next to the master bedroom would become the nursery. I could already see myself folding their tiny clothes in the walk-in closet. The room also had beautiful views of the mountains. Just imagining myself sitting on a soft rocking chair giving my baby a bottle as I looked out onto the Front Range made me feel very calm, hopeful, and peaceful.

8

THE UPHILL CLIMB
TO MOTHERHOOD

"The most magical day of my life was the day I became a parent."

—@PROUDHAPPYMAMA

As I looked around the empty nursery in our new home, I felt overwhelmed knowing that Rob and I had a massive metaphorical mountain to climb: how to have the children we wanted so badly.

We debated the pros and cons of adoption versus surrogacy. I started a spreadsheet to help us arrive at a logical solution for this deeply personal and emotional decision. I preferred to adopt until I investigated the rules and learned that agencies can reject you if you've had a serious illness like cancer. I was only a few years out of treatment, so there was still a possibility of a recurrence. On one level, I understand why adoption agencies wouldn't want to place a child with a person likely to die or get cancer. But the more I researched how the agencies did a comprehensive review of your health and medical history, the more bothered I became. I didn't like the idea of strangers judging whether I would live long enough to be a good parent. It felt unfair.

Ultimately, Rob and I chose surrogacy and egg donation. The biggest downside from my perspective was that this route was very expensive. Thankfully, because of Rob's business, we had the financial resources to afford this option. The other huge stumbling block I had about surrogacy was that Rob would be the only parent with a biological connection. I feared that our future children would not feel as connected to me. In hindsight, I know we are both equal parents no matter the genetics. At the time, however, it was just another reality to grieve.

I was also dealing with the residual feeling that Rob had made a huge sacrifice for me. After all, he could have chosen to marry someone who could bear his biological children. I struggled with this guilt throughout our entire quest to have children. Rob never made me feel bad. I knew it was my own issue, but it was emotionally charged.

• • •

To find a surrogate, we selected an agency called the Center for Surrogate Parenting (CSP). One of the requirements for people embarking upon the surrogacy journey was to write an essay describing our vision for our future family and why having children was important. I wrote about my experience with cancer, the devastating impact of infertility, and my lifelong dream to become a mom.

The agency warned us that it was typical to meet many potential surrogate candidates before finding "the one." It was a little like dating in this respect. Luck was on our side, though, because we found our match on the first try. CSP called to say they had a woman for us to meet, Katrese. She had read our story and wanted to meet us. We were invited to "interview" each other in the psychologist's office.

I was instantly drawn to Katrese and her husband, Chad. Katrese was in her early thirties but looked much younger. She even had braces! She was beautiful, with long, curly brown hair and deep brown eyes that sparkled when she smiled. She and Chad were obviously very much in love; they laughed and held hands, even finishing each other's sentences throughout our meeting.

The four of us hit it off so well that we ditched the psychologist's office and decided to continue talking over dinner at a local restaurant. We sat in a burgundy leather booth, and over a tower of onion rings, talked for more than three hours. To anyone who might have observed us, we looked like couples who had known each other for years. I shared more about my cancer story, and Katrese shared the pain of watching her friends go through infertility. Katrese and Chad's family was complete with two beautiful daughters, Breanna (age 8) and Caroline (age 4). Katrese loved being pregnant; it came easy to her. She explained that she had decided to become a surrogate, because she felt it was her calling to help another couple overcome infertility.

When Rob and I got in our car after dinner, we said in unison. "They're perfect!" Months later, we found out that Chad and Katrese said the same about us.

The process wasn't all smooth sailing. We still needed to find a second woman who would donate her eggs so that Katrese wouldn't have a genetic connection to the baby.

The egg donor search process was especially painful for me and once again triggered deep feelings of inadequacy. I grieved a lot during this period, tapping into still more pain that we couldn't bear children the "normal" way.

We worked with an egg donor agency, Fertility Futures, and were matched with a young college student who backed out a month into the process. I was disappointed but still determined. Here is what I visualized in my journal after this incident.

To my future baby,

You won't believe what I went through to get you. You are very special. You started as a dream. A wish. A longing.

It's been a long, tough road, and we've barely crossed the starting line. You are miles from us, but we will get to you. Eventually. Just keep plugging away. That's what I do. Filling the days, weeks, months, and years until you arrive. Keeping busy. Working, writing, running, are my main hobbies now. We found a surrogate mom to carry you to us. Katrese is wonderful. Better than I ever imagined. She's beautiful inside and out. Curly, chestnut brown hair down past her shoulder always styled halfway up with a barrette. She has a warm, caring smile. We can't wait to meet you.

Love,

Your Future Mom

Hope rose again when we were matched with a second egg donor. Unfortunately, after Katrese started the fertilization drugs, the donor suddenly got cold feet and quit. This time I was devastated. I cried for two days straight and couldn't sleep. For two different egg donors to flake out, my hope and optimism waned.

The egg donor process really tested our emotional resilience. I was determined to become a parent though and wasn't going to let *anything* stop me at this point.

It helped a lot that Katrese reassured us she would stick with us until we found the right egg donor. As we navigated a mix of anxiety and uncertainty, Katrese and Chad became two of our closest friends.

The third egg donor turned out to be our charm. What a relief! She followed through with her commitment and donated her eggs. This meant that Katrese could start a new cycle of hormones to become pregnant.

In-vitro fertilization, using donor eggs is a complicated scientific process. Once the eggs were donated, they had to be made into embryos. We waited five days for them to grow and become viable before they could be implanted into Katrese.

Chad, Rob, and I joined Katrese in the doctor's office on the day of the procedure. As she lay on the table, and we stood around her, Dr. Surrey wheeled in a futuristic-looking cart with a bright light shining in the middle of the clear box. "Here come the Guests of Honor!" he announced, referring to the two embryos. The four of us laughed nervously as he inserted both embryos into Katrese's uterus with a long dropper. Katrese was then instructed to rest in bed for a few days. All we could do next was wait for a miracle.

Would it work? What if it doesn't work? Can I handle more disappointment? The anxiety churned in my mind. The results were out of our control, and it was agonizing to sit on the sidelines and wait for the news.

My parents came to visit two weeks later. My mom and I were in Ulta Beauty, shopping in the shampoo aisle, trying to decide between the one for added volume or dry hair when my phone rang with Dr. Surrey's name on the screen. I motioned to my mom nervously and stepped aside to take the call. As I listened, I jumped up and down in the middle of the store and shouted, *"It worked! We're having TWINS!"* With tears of joy and disbelief, we dropped the shopping basket and left immediately. Katrese had become pregnant on the first try with both embryos. Miracles do happen. *I was finally going to be a mom.*

• • •

I was cautiously optimistic during the early weeks of Katrese's pregnancy. Anything could happen, especially with a high-risk twin pregnancy. I went to every doctor's appointment with her, feeling invisible each time the doctor ignored me and directed her comments to Katrese. "Hello!" I wanted to scream. *I'm the mother. I'm right here! Please talk to me.* Perhaps it was unintentional, but the whole experience only reinforced how different the road to parenthood was for me.

· · ·

One way I focused my energy that year was to train for a marathon. Running kept my nerves at bay and gave me a long-term goal to focus on. Unfortunately, two weeks before the marathon, I was on a twenty-three-mile practice run and busted my knee. This meant I couldn't complete the actual marathon after five months of training. Although this was very disappointing, I put it into perspective and kept my eye on the real prize that summer, becoming a mom.

When Katrese became pregnant, I quit my job to stop traveling. I wanted to be involved with doctor appointments and available to support her. I even envisioned helping take care of her young daughters if she felt tired and needed to rest.

I began researching all the supplies I'd need to become a twin mom—two cribs, a double stroller, two sets of clothes, two sets of bottles, two bassinets. During Katrese's third trimester, every day felt like a week. I became impatient for my turn to become a mom and to take care of our babies.

On August 19, 2005, the waiting abruptly ended. Six weeks before her October due date, Katrese developed a dangerous condition called pre-eclampsia. Giving birth was the only cure. Katrese selflessly resisted wanting to wait until the due date.

"No, the babies need more time," she begged. Chad, Rob, and I had to convince her to think about herself first. Rob and I didn't want her to be in any danger; we felt confident that our premature babies would be in good hands at Swedish Hospital.

Katrese was immediately hospitalized and scheduled to have a C-section the following morning. I stayed overnight on the plastic chair in her hospital room. We talked about how much the boys were loved already and how we dreamed them into this world. I was quivering with nerves, knowing I'd meet my two bundles the next day.

The sun came up on August 20th, and this morning was going to be one I'd always remember. Katrese and I took one last photo to show the contrast of her belly against mine (we had been doing side-by-side photos to document her growth during her entire pregnancy). Her silver braces caught the fluorescent light as she smiled, waved, and then followed a nurse into the operating room. Meanwhile, Chad, Rob, and I suited up in matching blue scrubs. We waited anxiously outside the operating room door with cellphones fully charged—ready to snap those all-important pictures and notify our equally anxious parents.

Thirty minutes later, the nurse cracked the door open. "We are ready for you," she said, signaling us to enter. I wasn't prepared for the sight of Katrese lying on the table, her abdomen splayed open. We were instructed to stand beside her head behind a green curtain erected at her neck. She smiled at us. *The surreal moment I'd been wishing for was finally here.*

My thoughts were interrupted by a beautiful cry. Baby A—we named him Jake—was lifted out of Katrese's belly. Jake was 4.4 pounds with a full head of black hair. Rob and I were hugging each other. We cut the umbilical cord, mesmerized, and watched the nurse rush him to the sink to clean and weigh him. Minutes later, Baby B joined us. Ryan weighed 5.6 pounds and had brown hair. Our two miracles were here, and I couldn't wait to hold them. But our joy quickly turned into fear when a frantic nurse yelled, "Get them to the NICU!"

"What's wrong?" I asked, terrified.

"He needs oxygen, STAT!" I heard another nurse yell. She put a large plastic mask over Ryan's face to deliver air. Jake breathed on his own.

The twins were quickly wrapped in the hospital's blue-and-pink-striped blankets. The nurses barked orders like military lieutenants. Rob was given Jake to hold, and I was given Ryan, with instructions to hold an oxygen mask tightly over his little face.

"Let's go—NOW!" two nurses said. They led a very nervous Rob and me, carrying these tiny, fragile babies, down a long hall to the Neonatal Intensive Care Unit (NICU).

No sooner did we enter the NICU than the nurses took the babies. We watched as they inserted feeding tubes into the boys' tiny nostrils. Ryan's portable oxygen mask was removed as he was transferred into an oxygen tank.

To our intense disappointment, we learned that they would need to stay in the hospital and be monitored 24/7. Their shared crib looked like a cage with metal bars. I was comforted, however, by the fact that they were together.

Rob's and my parents jumped on airplanes to meet their grandchildren for the first time. Minutes felt like hours in the NICU as we held the babies quietly in rocking chairs, watching for incremental improvements.

After the babies were settled and sleeping, we visited Katrese on a different floor of the hospital. She was sick from the heavy doses of magnesium given to women with pre-eclampsia. True to her character, Katrese was more concerned about the babies than about herself and committed to pumping and freezing her milk for the next six weeks to ensure the boys had the best possible nutrition.

The boys spent nearly three weeks in the NICU, and the days went by in a blur. We visited every day, sometimes spending up to twelve hours at a stretch. Rob set aside work during this period. He checked emails periodically, but mostly he was at the hospital with Jake and Ryan. There wasn't much we could do except hold the boys while they slept with feeding tubes and IV needles attached.

After nineteen days, Jake and Ryan were ready to come home. I'll never forget that morning. Pulling into the hospital for the final time, we parked our new navy-blue Honda Odyssey minivan in the spot designated for "new parents." Even that small detail felt monumental. I was no longer just a wife. I was a mother!

Entering the NICU for the last time was emotional. We had grown close to the nurses who cared for our babies. We hugged the entire staff, thanking them for guiding us to this life-changing moment.

We very carefully strapped Jake and Ryan into their car seats, driving no faster than five miles an hour the entire way home. We gingerly carried them upstairs to their new bedroom. The nursery was decorated in muted green and yellow tones, with a safari theme. Elephants and giraffes marched around walls and on the bumpers of their two cribs. The closet was full of newborn-sized clothes. The diaper table was stocked, and the kitchen counter brimmed with two sets of brand-new bottles and multiple cans of Similac baby formula.

As Rob and I laid the boys down into one shared crib. We stood there and quietly watched them breathe for a long time. Rob summed it up when, with wide eyes, he finally turned to me and asked, "So . . . what do we do now?"

And just like that, the heavy burden of infertility lifted. My dream had come true. Jake and Ryan were so worth the wait. Onto the next big adventure of parenthood—a path that promised to be full of love, adventure, triumphs, and tribulations.

9

NO COMPASS

"Embrace uncertainty. Some of the most beautiful chapters of our lives won't have a title until much later."

—BOB GOLLI

Before the boys arrived, I read enough how-to parenting books to fill a library. But actual parenting? It's altogether different. The first challenge was getting them on a sleep and feeding schedule that would allow us to sleep, too. We tried to keep the three-hour intervals established at the NICU, but we weren't too successful.

Due to their NICU experience and premature births, the boys were considered high-risk, so we went to our pediatrician weekly. Dr. Noah shared resources offered by the state for high-risk kids under three years old. Because of their expected developmental delays, it was determined that they both needed physical and occupational therapy starting at three to four months old.

The first year was a steep learning curve which I'm sure all new parents can relate to. I became efficient at diaper changing and did more loads of laundry in one year than I thought humanly possible. We relished watching the boys' development and documenting their milestones. When they each first rolled over, Rob and I cheered as if the Denver Broncos had won the Super Bowl.

At close to one year old, our occupational therapist noticed that Ryan had delayed speech. Through the supportive child services in Colorado, we found an amazing speech therapist, Laura, who came to our home.

One day, I was feeding Ryan in his highchair after his therapy session with Laura and casually mentioned that he had been squeezing his eyes open and shut. "Is this normal?" I asked. I was hyperaware of anything that didn't appear to be tracking in a typical way. In my Mommy & Me classes, it was hard not to notice that other babies of the same age were developing faster than Jake and Ryan.

"Has he ever had a seizure?" Laura asked.

Stunned, I replied, "What? No. Not that I know of." My heart dropped to the pit of my stomach.

"Maybe take him to an eye doctor . . ." she advised.

I made an appointment for the next week. As the doctor put dilation drops in his eyes, she asked me whether Ryan had ever had a stroke. Again, shocked. "No, never!" I responded. Just after the drops were put in, Ryan's right eye crossed and stuck there.

"Why are his eyes crossed?" I asked.

"Oh, that's normal. Once the drops wear off, his eyes will straighten again," she said reassuringly. The next day, Ryan's eyes were still crossed. Concerned, I called the eye doctor and went back to the office.

"Well, sometimes they stay crossed if they'd been wanting to cross before," she said nonchalantly. That made no sense to me, and I was upset. I learned the only cure for crossed eyes was glasses. We took both boys to get their eyes checked; it turned out they both needed glasses. Getting crawling babies to wear glasses was interesting.

When I mentioned that Ryan wasn't moving his right arm much, the ophthalmologist suddenly looked very serious. "You should see a neurologist immediately and get Ryan an MRI." Before leaving the office, I made an appointment at the Children's Hospital Colorado.

● ● ●

Due to continued developmental delays, the boys were in weekly therapy—physical therapy, occupational therapy, and speech. Since we had no family in town to help, our part-time nanny Natalei occasionally stayed overnight to give us a chance to catch up on sleep.

Rob and I took Ryan to the neurologist. After the MRI, the doctor said he would call with the results in a couple of days. For three days, we waited anxiously by the phone. When the call finally came, Natalei and I were acting out a silly Elmo puppet show for the boys. I excused myself and took the phone to another room.

"The MRI results came back. Your son has suffered a stroke," the doctor said. I don't think I heard anything after that bomb dropped.

"What . . . when . . . how?" I sputtered.

"We don't know," he said, "but it was a long time ago, possibly at birth or even before birth. You'll need to come back to the hospital and get a full work-up and tests done."

After I hung up, Natalei was the first person I told. We cried together on the floor, as the boys, oblivious, fought over the Elmo puppet.

When I collected myself, I called Rob, and he came home immediately. We knew our lives were about to take another dramatic turn into the unknown with no map or compass.

• • •

Soon, Rob and I were plunged headfirst into learning how a stroke affects babies. For the first time since my cancer treatment, I threw myself back into medical learning mode. Knowledge is power, and that's how I've always attempted to control the uncontrollable. I combed the Internet, studying everything I could about pediatric strokes. From the Johns Hopkins website, I learned that pediatric stroke is a rare condition, affecting one in every 4,000 newborns and an additional 2,000 older children each year.

Despite medical advances, when we asked our first neurologist about how the stroke would impact Ryan cognitively, he said starkly, "We don't know. You will find out whether Ryan can say his name and phone number in the first grade." This was terrifying. Concern about Ryan's cognitive, emotional, and physical development consumed us during his baby and toddler years.

We added feeding therapy to the long list of interventions since it was hard for Ryan to chew. At two years old, he was very underweight. We fed him Ensure every day and gave him the highest-calorie foods. Finally, he gained weight. Thank goodness both boys started walking at eighteen to twenty-one months, because they were getting too heavy to carry!

It was a challenge to manage both kids' feeding, bathing, and napping schedules, along with Ryan's medical needs. Some days felt endless, yet through it all, I felt tremendous gratitude and joy in taking care of them. We took frequent field trips to the zoo, museums, the mall, and went to Mommy & Me classes and for walks. Getting the boys ready for outings in their side-by-side double stroller was like planning a complicated military maneuver. Bottles? Check. Diapers? Check. Wipes? Check. Snacks? Check. Change of clothes in case of accident? Check! I loved to dress them in coordinated outfits. They were good sports. I took photos of them constantly—probably thousands in those first two years alone. They were so cute, and I would often pinch myself, wondering, *Is this real?*

Ryan has a lively personality. In fact, as a child, he was either laughing maniacally or crying hysterically. Jake, by comparison, was calm, steady, and mellow. I marveled at their different personalities and how they balanced each other perfectly. To this day, Jake is more serious, and Ryan is very expressive.

• • •

For Rob and me, our lives were especially hectic those years. Our conversations became all about the kids, the house, work, and the logistics of living. Not surprisingly, intimacy in our marriage waned. Rob and I started to drift apart, but I didn't want to pay attention to the fissures in our marriage just yet. We were exhausted, working our hardest, and Rob was devoting every spare second to the kids and his growing business.

In hindsight, I realize how easy it is to sweep problems under the rug when the towering press of daily life feels overpowering. I was simply too preoccupied with mothering twins to pay closer attention to the lack of connection affecting our marriage.

PART IV:

FINDING
MY PURPOSE

10

A HEALING ODYSSEY

"To heal our wounds, we need the courage to face them."

—PAULO COELHO

Several years post cancer, I was still struggling with fears of a recurrence. I'd dodged a bullet by surviving and wondered when (not if) it would come back. For many of us, survivorship means to live in cancer's dark shadow, hoping it won't snatch us again.

Shortly before the boys were born, I was invited to a weekend program for women cancer survivors, Healing Odyssey, located in Malibu, California. The program was started in 1993 by Nancy Raymon, an oncology nurse specialist, and Donna Farris, a clinical social worker, to help women heal from their cancer experiences. The weekend more than lived up to its name. It transformed my self-limiting beliefs, challenged my fears, and emboldened me to go forward.

Leslie Sinclair was the first person I met when I arrived at camp. With her short, spunky red hair and deep, hazel eyes, she radiated warmth and understanding. Only twenty-three years old, she had more empathy than people decades older. A former camp participant, Leslie fell in love with the retreat's life-changing program and had decided to give back as a volunteer camp counselor.

There were thirty women of all ages, mostly older than me (except Leslie), and most from Los Angeles and Orange County. (Only a few people, like me, had flown in from out of state.) When everyone arrived, we sat in a circle and introduced ourselves. *Why were we there?* Cancer survivors realize time is precious and tend to skip the small talk. *What did we want to get from the experience?* At first, it was hard opening myself up to a group of strangers. But as woman after woman began to speak, I started to relax and trust. We'd all been through a similar war, and although the details were different, many of the emotions were the same. We bonded through our shared experiences of fear, pain, anxiety, and most importantly, our determination to heal ourselves.

The next morning was our first mysterious adventure. Split into groups of fifteen, we were driven in a large van to the middle of the forest. Weaving through the trees, I was curious about where they were taking us and why. As the van came to a stop, my eyes fixed on a log suspended high in the sky between two tall, thin trees. Looking up, the log was about three stories high and fifty feet long.

Is this a joke?

Gathering around, we met Cathy, our "warrior" instructor, decked out in a pair of serious hiking boots. She welcomed us to the "Log Climb Challenge" and instructed us to put on a harness before climbing the rickety ladder leaning against one of the trees. Once at the top, we were to walk across the log until we reached the other tree. Only then could we sit back in our harness and be lowered to the ground.

When I imagined trying to balance and walk across a rounded log like a tightrope, I thought ... no thank you. I'll pass. I was sure the others felt the same. But to my amazement, the women (many bald and undergoing chemotherapy) lined up to attempt what seemed to me to be an impossible task. Their bravery inspired me. My pulse quickened when it was my turn, but the women encouraged me. I was too nervous to make my fingers work properly, so Cathy helped fasten the harness on tight. With sweaty palms and shaky legs, I inched my way up the ladder. I froze at the top rung, hugging the tree for dear life.

From forty feet below, about three stories of a house, came Cathy's reassuring voice. "You made it to the top, now LET GO and walk across."

"I can't do this," I shouted.

"Yes, you can." I heard the chorus of voices respond. "You can do this, Marcia!" I looked down again, nearly crying from fear, and saw my fellow campers' faces. They looked impossibly small down there. Next Leslie's voice pierced through with conviction. "Trust yourself." The group joined in and repeated the mantra.

After several minutes that felt like hours, going back down the ladder was not an option. I let go of the ladder and stepped out onto the rounded log. My focus narrowed in to find balance without anything to hold onto. With arms outstretched, I took tiny, halting steps away from the safety of the tree. The present moment was sharp and full of clarity. I willed myself to inch forward, one tiny step at a time.

When I made it to the other side, heart beating out of my chest, I leaned back into the harness, trusting it would catch me—and it did. Back on solid ground, I felt immense relief and sheer exhilaration— how had I, someone with a fear of heights, managed to walk across a thin log suspended three stories off the ground? I felt an intoxicating surge of confidence and surprising power over my fears.

My pride was short-lived.

Little did I know what was in store for us next. That afternoon, we were all driven high atop a 2,000-foot cliff overlooking Malibu Forest. This time we were greeted by a rugged guide named Bill, who looked like a real cowboy next to his red Ford truck. He held a stack of more dreaded harnesses.

It was then that I spotted a long wooden plank hanging off the cliff. *What in the world…?* I thought to myself. "Welcome to the Edge," Bill said with a dramatic pause. "Here's what's going to happen. One at a time, I will put a harness around your shoulders and a rope around your waist. Once the equipment is secured, I will guide you off the cliff to the edge of the plank, where you will dangle your toes. Your mission, if you choose to accept it, is to lean forward—all the way forward—until you completely let go. Only then will I pull you back to stable ground."

"*Oh, hell no,*" I thought as I gazed 2,000 feet down to the valley floor. My mind raced, searching for any plausible excuse to get out of this. The earlier exercise had only *felt* like suicide. This would be suicidal, I was convinced. One thing was sure: I didn't survive cancer to die like this.

Bill asked for a volunteer, and thankfully, a brave soul raised her hand. If I hadn't been aware yet how courageous this group of women was, I was now beginning to grasp it. Just as before, one by one, everyone did the exercise while the rest of us watched in terror. When it was my turn, I, once again, wanted to run the other way but coaxed myself to be brave like the others. Bill tied the rope around my waist and secured the harness on my shoulders. Somehow, I forced my steps onto the plank of death as Bill walked behind me, whispering encouragement. "A little more, a little more, a little more." I have never been more scared in my entire life.

With each step, I imagined falling to my untimely death. My funeral. My poor parents' anguish. The other women were silent, sensing I needed this space to confront my overwhelming fears.

In tears, I panicked at the edge and begged Bill to let me go back to solid ground. There was no turning back. "You can do this," he insisted. "Lean forward and let yourself fall."

I stared over the abyss and convinced myself to *let go*. Let go of what? Let go of control, trying to control everything. In that moment, I did it. I gave in to the feeling of being totally and completely out of control. I may die. I may not. Believe. Trust. As I let go of control, I felt like I was flying over the plank, over the cliff, and over the valley. The fear was primal and intense. I roared out the pervasive agony caused by my cancer, my divorce, my infertility, my failures, my losses, my grief. Tears streamed down my face as Bill finally pulled me back to reality and hugged me tightly to calm my nerves.

I was sweaty, physically shaking, and wildly euphoric. Leslie removed my harness, and my pulsing heart began to slow down. The other women surrounded me with supportive hugs and high-fives as they did for every person releasing their deepest fears into the Malibu canyon's deep valley.

The Edge experience changed me. I had taken on my fear of dying and told it to go to hell. The Healing Odyssey experiences restored faith in my body and in my own courage. Most importantly, Leslie became a dear friend. After the camp, I joined her email list of hundreds of people whom she updated periodically about her ongoing battle with cancer. I pledged to support her through the cruel and unpredictable hell called cancer.

• • •

Back home, it was an impossible task to track Leslie's progress through her emails. As I struggled to remember which doctor's visit was coming up and which protocol she had finished, I couldn't help but think that one consolidated website would allow her friends to better follow her progress. I imagined how one place to post information on her latest treatments would be easier for her friends to access without having to sift through dozens of emails to keep track. The more I thought about it, the more I realized there was indeed a better way to help Leslie communicate and connect with her loved ones.

Life was too busy for me to flesh out or act on this germ of an idea, but ever so slowly, it began to take shape in my mind.

11

BIRTHING A LIFELINE FOR OTHERS

"Service to others is the rent you pay for a room here on earth."

—MOHAMMAD ALI

Fast forward to 2006 when the boys are almost one year old. I was knee-deep in diapers and soft rubber toys. I found motherhood fulfilling, awe-inspiring, and at times, a little mindless. Everything took twice as long with twins. Even giving them bottles took about forty-five minutes for each baby. Sometimes I would think to myself, *I went to college! I know how to solve complex equations!* Other days, I would remember leaning dangerously off a plank in the Malibu hills, wearing a harness, armed only with faith that I would survive.

The days were full of mundane activities like blending applesauce, following my kids with a vacuum, and washing spit from our clothes. Who had I become? Professional laundry woman, puree-er, and toy cleaner?

If any of this resonates with you, know that you are not alone. And that you are not a bad parent (just an honest one). The truth is,

I loved my boys with every cell in my body. And yet I also missed working in the professional world to challenge my mind. I missed problem-solving on the job. Bantering with colleagues. Dressing up for work and not looking like I'd gotten into a fight with my blender or vacuum cleaner.

I'd worked since I was fourteen years old and felt good about myself when advancing my career.

After my cancer experience, I knew I wanted to make a difference in the lives of other cancer patients. That's why I had volunteered for years before the boys were born as a resource coordinator at the Anschutz Cancer Center at the University of Colorado Hospital. Perched in the small library next to the oncology waiting room, I shared important resources with family members pacing anxiously while their loved ones visited the oncology team. Whether they needed a listening ear, support group, transportation, financial support, or educational materials, I offered solutions. Serving others in this way felt meaningful and something I could be proud of, and I missed that feeling.

As I was feeding the boys or putting them down for naps, my mind was restless with ideas on how I could create a meaningful career that was flexible around raising young children. Gearing up for my "What's next?" another career reset was percolating in my mind.

• • •

Before the boys were born, even before the beginning of my surrogacy journey, I had become a de facto "cancer whisperer." Friends undergoing cancer treatment, and friends of friends, turned to me for guidance and advice. I was happy to provide any help I could, knowing firsthand how debilitating cancer treatment can be mentally, physically, emotionally, and spiritually.

Ironically, playing the role of cancer guide was second nature to me. I was a psychology major in college because I loved learning about people and what makes them tick. I'm interested in what drives people to make the choices they do. I've always enjoyed helping people—be it the passengers on my American Airlines flights or my CEO clients at the tech company I worked for.

One day in 2003, I met Lori Arquilla Andersen, who changed my life. Lori, also thirty-three at the time, was introduced to me by a mutual friend after being diagnosed with brain cancer. Lori's diagnosis happened six years after my own cancer experience. Her friends Shannon and Tony owned a web development company and created a website for Lori to easily connect with loved ones during her cancer journey. I stayed in close contact with Lori through her website and remember wishing that I'd had such a powerful tool when I was dealing with my own cancer. Keeping my friends and family up to date had been an enormous struggle. I felt guilty for not returning calls or responding to emails quickly enough, but both tasks exhausted me. I also found it incredibly depressing to repeat the same details of my situation to different people.

Lori had been able to easily update family and friends through her website, and I noted what a profound difference this made not only for her but for everyone in her life. The website even had tools for people to sign up to offer help, from giving rides to medical appointments to dropping off meals when she needed them.

Tragically, Lori passed away two years after her diagnosis, at the age of thirty-five. This was the summer my boys were born. It was a terrible irony that as I was celebrating my babies' new lives, her young life was ending. After she died, I could not stop thinking about her or what her grieving mother said to me: "*That website was our lifeline.*"

Lifeline. Lifeline. The word stuck in my head. *Every family impacted by cancer should have a lifeline.*

I would find myself thinking of Lori's *lifeline* at the oddest times— as I loaded another pile of baby clothes into the machine, or when I was going over the next day's grocery list. Although I was knee-deep in diapers and feeding schedules, I knew that the idea of an online community dedicated to the specific needs of cancer patients and their loved ones could make a huge impact on their lives.

I also knew that this was the exact thing that could help my dear friend Leslie Sinclair. As I mentioned earlier, Leslie from Healing Odyssey had literally hundreds of people on her email list. When responding to her posts, many of these people would hit REPLY ALL. One day, I woke up to about 200 email responses from Leslie's friends and supporters. There had to be a better way! I knew that if I wanted to see that happen, it was up to me to do it.

• • •

The idea of starting a lifeline for cancer patients continued to obsess me. Finally, in 2006, a year after Lori passed away and when my boys were a year old, I decided to start a nonprofit organization called MyLifeLine in memory of Lori and in honor of Leslie and her incredible courage.

It might sound crazy to start a nonprofit organization when you have year-old twins. But it's also crazy to ignore your inner voice when it's shouting at you loud and clear. Plus, I sensed deep down that I would be a better mother and person if I was happy doing fulfilling professional work. I wanted to find a way to combine motherhood and work, and even if it was going to be messy, I would give it my best shot.

Let me be clear: I knew nothing about creating a nonprofit organization. Thankfully, this did not stop me. After all, this wasn't the first time I ventured into new territory. I'd done it to become a flight attendant and then again when I became a regional sales manager at a large computer distributor. Because I love to learn and research, I taught myself what I needed to know—and sought help and counsel for everything else. During my boys' naptime, mapping out MyLife-Line challenged my mind and got me back into the workforce on my own terms.

Initially, I thought of MyLifeLine as a creative project that would benefit others. Little did I know how much work this philanthropic endeavor would entail. I had no idea that building a nonprofit is as challenging as creating any other type of business. For some reason, there seems to be a myth that setting up a nonprofit is easier. But trust me, it isn't.

As they say, ignorance is bliss. I jumped in, feet first. Devouring everything I could about how to build a nonprofit, I reached out to every savvy person I knew. I did research online and gathered a close group of caring, smart friends together to create a board of directors, including Katrese and her sister Monique. We hired an IT developer who was a cancer survivor and helped us think through important website features for the cancer journey. As a Board, we wrote and rewrote the business and marketing plans.

Together, we proudly launched MyLifeLine.org Cancer Foundation in 2007 with a vision to transform the cancer experience through community and connection.

It was a wild, exciting ride to be raising young boys and building a nonprofit business at the same time. I'll never forget having to rush to a business meeting after dropping my boys at home after a swim lesson. I didn't have time to change my handbag, and while I left the swim bag with their wet suits at home, somehow one of the boys' diapers ended up poking out of the top of my laptop bag. People in the meeting graciously pointed out the diaper with the Elmo drawings on the elastic waistband, and we had a good laugh.

A somewhat mortifying episode occurred when the boys were three. We were on a plane headed to Philadelphia to stay with Rob's parents. I'd planned to leave the boys with them so that I could present MyLifeLine to oncology professionals at the Fox Chase Cancer Center. One of my suitcases was filled with diapers, toys and clothes, and the other had marketing materials for the meeting.

As you know, I am a former flight attendant, a flying veteran. Two toddler boys in a plane for four hours? How hard could it be? Piece of cake, I thought. Um. Not this time.

An hour into our flight, Jake began to throw up. Profusely. Poor Jake! I was trying to keep Ryan away to prevent him from catching whatever bug Jake had. While trying to comfort Jake, it was a challenge to accurately aim vomit into the paper bag provided (and not end up covered in vomit myself). Sorry for the visual.

My hair turned gray in those four hours. Things reached their climax when I realized a) I had to go to the bathroom, and b) the boys' diapers needed changing. No way was I going to subject my fellow passengers not only to the smell of Jake's vomit but also to the smells (and sights) of their dirty diapers.

Have you ever tried going to the bathroom on a plane with two screaming toddlers wedged in with you? Worse, have you tried to change a baby's diaper in one of those tiny bathrooms? Or two babies' diapers? There was not enough space to plop either of them down near the tiny sink (not that I would have anyways, being paranoid about germs), so I had to do it bending over while they stood up. I'll leave the details to your imagination, but let's just say it wasn't pretty.

We finally landed in Philadelphia, but I tell this story as one of my parenting highlights (and if you're a parent, I know you have stories of your own). Flying with sick toddlers and days spent tripping over and picking up scattered toys for the twentieth time—these are the less-talked-about and certainly less glamorous aspects of parenting.

• • •

Despite the challenges of balancing a new career and raising young children, I truly believe that I am a better mother because of my work and a better worker because of my kids. Parenting strengths of empathy and organization of chaos can be essential as a leader. And the skills I use at work (big picture thinking, humor, and strategy— as anyone who has ever negotiated bedtime with a four-year-old will know) are also essential parenting skills.

Looking back on those hectic years where everything was learn-on-the-go, I know that frazzled as I was, I grew exponentially as an individual, a nonprofit leader, and most importantly, as a mother. I miss those days now that my boys are teenagers.

12

COMMUNITY TAKES A VILLAGE

"My parents are my backbone. Still are. They're the only ones that still support you if you score zero or forty."

—KOBE BRYANT

None of MyLifeLine's growth would have been possible without the support of my friends and family. And specifically, my amazing parents. They have been deeply involved in MyLifeLine ever since its founding. In fact, I don't think it's an overstatement to say that the organization would not exist in its current form without them. My own cancer diagnosis made them feel helpless; supporting MyLifeLine gave them the ability to do something concrete to make a difference.

Mom and Dad have not only never missed a single fundraiser, but they have also come to conferences, stayed up late xeroxing and emailing and dealing with everything from computer snafus to helping with the kids. In the early days, both my mom and dad accompanied me to oncology and medical conferences, and this is where they truly shone. They were the "Dynamic Duo," connecting with nurses, social workers, and doctors, year after year, tirelessly promoting MyLifeLine's services with healthcare workers.

I'll never forget our first tradeshow for MyLifeLine at McCormick Place, a huge conference center in Chicago. It was 2008, one year after MyLifeLine was launched. This annual June conference is hosted by the American Society of Clinical Oncologists and is one of the largest conferences in the yearly calendar. Over 30,000 oncology professionals come from all around the world. In addition, all the big pharmaceutical companies attend, with million-dollar booths set up front and center in the conference hall. They entice doctors and cancer professionals with their big-screen televisions, gleaming cappuccino machines, and ice cream cone and dessert stations, to say nothing of the free swag (everything from T-shirts and pens to caps and water bottles).

This was the one trade show my mom couldn't attend, so Dad and I walked in, dazzled by the bright lights and noise. Holding a single brown box of MyLifeLine materials, we made our way to the back of the room, into the small dark corner where our ten-by-ten-foot stand was designated. Dad helped me hang our MyLifeLine banner on the curtain behind us. Our little square of carpet was slightly threadbare, but we didn't care. We were so excited to be there and to be sharing the message of MyLifeLine with everyone we could.

Dad and I fanned out my business cards and pens with the MyLifeLine logos and scattered Hershey's kisses to help attract hungry attendees. But none of it would have mattered if it weren't for my dad, who went to work on the crowd immediately. "Have you heard of MyLifeLine for your patients?" he would ask of literally everyone who passed our booth.

Let me add here that my dad is the type of person who makes friends everywhere he goes. I know this is a cliché, but with him, it is true. He is a social worker who spent most of his career with the child welfare department of Orange County. My entire life, I have seen him working tirelessly to help others. When I was a kid, my dad would sleep with an emergency pager on his nightstand. In the middle of many nights, he would get summoned to rescue children who were suspected of being abused or in danger.

At our first American Society of Clinical Oncology (ASCO) conference, no one had heard of MyLifeLine, but my dad's incredible warmth and charm made people stop and listen. He wasn't even fazed by people who just stopped to scoop up a pen and some chocolates. Dad just kept at it, talking and schmoozing, ultimately winning over anyone who spent more than thirty seconds with him. He manages to find commonalities with everyone.

"My daughter is a cancer survivor and started this organization!" he would boast to everyone who stopped for a free pen. Not only was I touched by his pride in me, but I quickly realized that his telling others my cancer story gave me "street cred." At the conference, we built up our email list to stay in touch with the oncology doctors and clinicians. When we returned home, I immediately went to work, reaching out to begin creating strategic partnerships with cancer centers.

Two groups of people that both my mother and my father were an especially big hit with were the oncology nurses and social workers. At later conferences catering to these groups, the nurses and social workers fell in love with my parents and what MyLifeLine could do for their patients. It didn't hurt that my dad told the oncology social workers that he was a social worker, too. The nurses and social workers really "got" us, and these were the conferences we loved the most.

We had a family routine. While my dad did the schmoozing, my mother and I would try to catch others passing the booth. My mother is warm and sweet, and people love her as well, but she is more reserved, while my dad is a true extrovert. Together, though, we were an unstoppable team.

13

FINDING COURAGE, PURPOSE, AND HOPE

"When we live it all on purpose, though . . . when we make it all matter . . . that is wonderfully courageous."

—AMBER HAVEKOST, MYLIFELINE MEMBER
& BREAST CANCER SURVIVOR

Building MyLifeLine Cancer Foundation was a massive team effort, something I never could have done alone. Together, with a small army of dedicated family and friends, we structured an organization from the ground up, designed our online community platform, launched fundraising campaigns and events, built strategic healthcare partnerships, and connected with cancer patients, caregivers, and oncology professionals to offer our program nationwide.

I am especially grateful to the extraordinary people I met along the way. The generous board members. Tireless volunteers and staff. And brave cancer survivors and caregivers who joined MyLifeLine's community. I have been inspired and changed by all of them.

When I think of courage, Burke Ryder is the first to come to mind. Growing up in Breckenridge, Colorado, Burke was an active kid—he learned to ski before he could walk and started racing by the age of eight as a member of Breckenridge's Alpine Racing Team. But cancer knows no boundaries, not even for thirteen-year-old boys.

"Burke always loved to ski and climb and hike," said his father, Lee Ryder. "One October, he was in training, and the team was running up Breckenridge Mountain. Burke told me his leg was hurting him afterwards. I teased him and said it was because he was out of shape."

"Soon after that, we had a routine pediatrician appointment," said his mom, Kristin. The doctor urged Burke to get an X-ray on his leg. Within half an hour, he called Kristin and Lee and told them their son had some sort of tumor, and he didn't know for sure, but it was probably cancerous. "Our whole world was turned upside down almost instantaneously. It was a complete shock," said Kristin.

Burke was diagnosed with osteosarcoma in October of 2017. This talented, young athlete eventually needed his leg amputated to save his life. Everyone in the family was impacted, of course, including Teo, Burke's younger brother. "Everyone had to be courageous, but it was pretty scary," Teo said. "Cancer can be a really tough thing."

"The first week when we received Burke's diagnosis, we were overwhelmed with people who wanted to help," said Kristin. "Then a friend told me about MyLifeLine. It was one way Burke could send out information, and I could ask for help and keep everyone in the loop. It was a gift—I didn't have to answer a thousand phone calls, and people could find out in real time how to support us."

"Our motto through this whole ordeal was—and still is— 'you got this," said Kristin. "People would let Burke know through MyLife-Line how strong he was. MyLifeLine has kept us going. For us to know so many people have our backs is incredible."

The Ryder family received MyLifeLine's *Courage Award* in 2019 at our annual fundraising event. The 250-strong audience shouted out to the family on stage as he accepted the award, "*Burke, you got this!*" There was not a dry eye in the house as Burke soaked in the love from the crowd. Still, mom Kristin insists that the award is all Burke's. "He's the courageous one. The *Courage Award* goes to him."

On November 10, 2022, Burke sadly died at home surrounded by his loving family. Burke had been a senior at the school he loved, Kimball Union Academy, in New Hampshire. In addition to being an exceptional student leader, Burke continued to brave more clinical trials demonstrating heroic levels of resilience and courage. His parents used MyLifeLine to notify Burke's support community that he passed away peacefully. The entire family is a powerful inspiration to all who know them, and Burke will never be forgotten.

When I reflect about purpose, I think of Amber Havekost, a friend diagnosed with advanced breast cancer in her late 30's in August 2017. Amber found therapeutic relief in authentically documenting her painful journey on MyLifeLine's platform daily for four years. Her husband and three teenage daughters have supported her every step of the way.

"We've navigated nearly 300 medical appointments and met almost 230 different medical professionals, all while making some of the most important decisions of our lives," Amber recalled. "MyLife-Line's Helping Calendar, as well as resources for both patients and caregivers, have been so important for us. The most significant part of MyLifeLine has been my personal blog, where I have been able to write and process this monster of a journey. I've written nearly 1,500 posts since my diagnosis." Amber says that MyLifeline reminded her that "community is way stronger than cancer." Today, Amber serves other survivors as a grief and trauma coach encouraging them to create power and meaning by courageously and authentically processing their own journeys and inspiring them to live on purpose.

When I think of making it all matter, the story of Jen Garza and Britton Thomas rises to the top. In 2009, Britton's wife Jacqueline ("Jax") Arcaris was diagnosed with an aggressive form of breast cancer. Around that same time, in a different part of the country, Jen fell in love with and married Ruben Garza, a young cancer survivor battling Hodgkin's lymphoma. Both couples used MyLifeLine to keep friends and family updated throughout their respective treatments. In late 2011, Ruben passed away at the age of 37. Jax died the following year not long after marking her 40th birthday. Knowing that Jen and Britton were grieving at the same time, I emailed Jen to ask if she would be open to corresponding with Britton, who desperately needed to connect with someone he could relate to. Correspondence was slow to start, but gradually Jen and Britton began reaching out to each other via email for advice during the hardest times. "How did you get through the first wedding you attended after he died?" "What was I supposed to wish for when I blew my birthday candles out and my only wish couldn't come true?"

Soon after Ruben's death, Jen fulfilled a long-held dream of her late husband's. She decided to go see the band My Morning Jacket at Red Rocks Amphitheatre in Colorado. She bought two tickets, not knowing whom she would invite to accompany her. She also booked a skydiving trip for the same day. Then she remembered that Britton lived somewhere in Colorado. Jen told him about the skydiving and the concert, and he decided to join her.

"Just before skydiving," Jen recalled, "we both realized we were terrified of losing our wedding rings, so we went out to the car to nervously lock them away. We shared an understanding. When the cameraman responsible for filming and documenting our adventure asked us why we were skydiving, we answered in our own ways but expressed the same sentiment. We had people we needed to get closer to up there."

Neither Jen nor Britton had any expectations of romance at that point, but both felt something taking root that night at the concert. After a full moon rose behind the stage, Jen whispered to Britton, "Ruben is somehow here tonight. He would have found so many things about this show magical. The only thing missing is fireworks—he loved fireworks." As Jen remembers it, within moments, fireworks appeared off in the distance—in early August! "It felt like Ruben and Jax choreographed the evening, serving us beautiful moment after beautiful moment."

"Later," Jen recalled, "when it came time to say goodbye, it was much harder than either of us expected—we hugged and couldn't let go, and that was the beginning ..."

Jen flew home to Austin, Texas, and read all forty of Jax's MyLifeLine blog pages. And Britton read Jen's posts. The more they read, the more they felt that if they had known Jax and Ruben, they would have been friends.

Jen and Britton started a long-distance relationship until it was clear that they were meant to be together. Britton moved from Denver to Austin to be closer to Jen and proposed in October 2014. In lieu of wedding favors, the couple donated to MyLifeLine in loving memory of Jax and Ruben.

"Jax and Ruben will always be a part of our lives," said Britton. "We aren't replacing them because they can never be replaced. But there's a new chapter now. There IS a future." There is indeed. Jen and Britton moved back to Colorado where sparks between them first flew. They are now happily married, live in the mountains as they always dreamed, and are raising two young daughters.

Inspired by Jen and Britton's remarkable story of hope, MyLifeLine launched the #Ribboning Challenge on Instagram in 2015. The challenge? Take a photo of yourself in a ribbon shape (arms overhead with fingers touching, and legs spread wide like the bottom of a cancer ribbon). Then, post and tag someone fighting cancer to show your support on social media. Photos tagging survivors poured in from countries all over the world (even Antarctica!) and across all fifty states of the USA. We were amazed by the creativity—photos showed people #ribboning while skydiving, scuba diving, on tops of famous monuments and bridges, on beaches, planes, and snow-covered mountains. Baseball teams and fashion designers even joined the challenge. Soon, the media took notice. People Magazine published an article on its website on July 16, 2015 titled "How the #Ribboning Social Campaign Aims to Humanize the Cancer Journey." And when Jen and Britton's wedding photo (with both of them in ribboning poses) was broadcast on New York's biggest screen in Times Square, MyLifeLine was given exposure on the *Good Morning America* set.

#Ribboning had exceeded our wildest expectations. Colorado Governor John Hickenlooper even declared July 16, 2016, a statewide day of #Ribboning to honor those impacted by cancer.

I still marvel at the many "kismet" experiences brought about by the people in MyLifeLine's community. One morning in March 2010, I was reading *The Denver Post* while having breakfast. I nearly choked on my oatmeal when I saw MyLifeLine mentioned on the front page. George Karl, then NBA head coach of the Denver Nuggets, had been diagnosed with cancer, and he was using MyLifeLine to communicate his progress during treatment. I hadn't even known that Coach Karl had cancer, much less that his family was using MyLifeLine.

Within hours after the article appeared, our web servers almost crashed due to the heavy traffic. The Nuggets were headed into the NBA playoffs, bringing an even greater urgency to Coach Karl's story.

In the years that followed, Coach Karl (aka George) and his partner, Kim, became good friends in addition to MyLifeLine ambassadors, board members, donors, sponsors—and our biggest cheerleaders. George has been instrumental in helping spread the word about MyLifeLine beyond Colorado and long after he left the Denver Nuggets.

While several of my personal inspirations are mentioned in this chapter and book, there are countless others who have been mentors guiding me forward. One thing I believe is the *only* thing that will matter in the end is the quality of our relationships. When we connect with those sharing our purpose, our days will be inspired by courage and hope.

14

ON MY OWN AGAIN

"Much of life is about failure, whether we acknowledge it or not, and your destiny is profoundly shaped by how effectively you learn from and adapt to failure."

—DAVID BROOKS

In 2014, seven years after starting MyLifeLine, I needed to step back and take a breath. The boys were now in second grade and needed me in new and different ways. I was worn out from the demands of running a nonprofit organization, especially the endless fundraising. We found a new executive director that we hoped could take the organization to the next level. I was relieved because I desperately needed to find some balance in my life. I had begun to worry about my physical and mental well-being.

Between Rob's demanding career and my own and the sheer hecticness of life with two children, we lost our connection as a couple. As I mentioned earlier, the cracks in our relationship had begun when the kids were little.

Rob's business was thriving. I offered to help, yet he always turned me down. I was disappointed he didn't take me up on my offer because I thought this would bring us closer. I yearned for a deeper spiritual and emotional partnership with Rob, but every time I tried to pry this door open, he closed it. "Let's talk about it later . . . ." This became a mantra, and not surprisingly, later never came. I felt very lonely. This was a familiar feeling from my first marriage and an ominous sign that things were very much going in the wrong direction.

One day, during a routine annual cancer checkup, I found myself reflecting on my life. I was always aware of living on borrowed time, so each time cancer scans came back negative, I felt true relief. Clean scans also underscored for me that I wanted to reach my highest potential while I still had time. Another year until the next scan! I was free. What was I going to do over the next year, two years, or forty years? Was I going to be fulfilled? Happy? More immediately, I wondered, were Rob and I still going to be married?

Our marriage had become all business. The lightbulb went off after this cancer scan: we were simply not compatible. Staying in a marriage lacking intimacy and connection would kill me if the cancer didn't come back first.

• • •

After years of therapy, we were at a standstill. Together, we realized how unhappy we were and discussed our options. While we were both very sad and hurt, we made an excruciating decision to end the marriage. After that, things moved swiftly. We didn't need lawyers, only a mediator. Our divorce became official in March 2014 just five months after the decision. One thing I am proud of is that we were kind to each other. We went to a child advocate who walked us through creating our custody and child agreement. Everything we did was centered on Jake and Ryan and easing this difficult path for them as much as possible. They were only eight years old.

The night we told the boys was one of the worst nights of my life. We invited them to the basement for what we called a "family meeting."

Rob nodded in my direction, so I started. "We love you very, very much. But Dad and I have decided we would be better apart than together." A moment of stunned silence. Before I could get another word out, Ryan screamed out in pain understanding the crushing weight of this news. Jake looked at Ryan, taking his cue, and screamed next. Within moments, Rob and I were surrounded by ear-splitting wailing in stereo.

Before the talk, our plan was to stay calm no matter what happened, so the boys would know that everything would be OK. We hugged them tightly, reassuring them over and over that we would still be their parents, we would still love them, and most importantly, that none of this was their fault.

Trying to lighten the mood, I eventually said, "Let's go upstairs for mac & cheese!" Food, luckily, was the perfect distraction. They bounded upstairs and even smiled when I put the steaming bowls of Kraft in front of them. Then, suddenly, Ryan remembered the news and screamed out in despair. He dropped his head and sobbed. We were all heartbroken.

Rob and I held ourselves together until the boys went to bed. After they were asleep, we went into our own room and cried together the rest of the night. I was wracked with guilt and wondered if we had just completely ruined their lives. And yet, at the same time, I knew in my heart that we had given this marriage all we had, but we just couldn't get on the same page. It was better to acknowledge this fact head-on, as painful as it was. Rob and I would do everything to make sure the boys would continue to feel secure and loved.

Getting divorced for the second time was humiliating and not how I envisioned my life. I felt ashamed of myself and devastated for my children. Still, I had to forge ahead. We had made the right decision. Both of us deserved to be with partners with whom we could deeply connect on all levels.

I had survived so much already; I would survive this loss, too.

• • •

When the divorce was official, I moved out of our shared home. While I had assumed I'd move to a small apartment since I earned a modest income, Rob insisted on buying me a home just two blocks away, so the boys could walk back and forth between us. Like I said, he is a very generous man and a tremendous father. Those things never changed.

Life as a single mom is challenging. My work needed to be flexible and accommodate the kids' school and summer schedules. MyLife-Line hired a full-time executive director, and we created a part-time role for me as the chief mission officer helping as a spokesperson responsible for fundraising and outreach. This position was perfect as it empowered me to juggle home, parenting, and work priorities. As stressful as some days were, I was grateful to have this opportunity to try and "do it all."

But like my friend, Annie, once told me, "You can have it all. Just not all at the same time."

15

THE URGE TO MERGE

"If opportunity doesn't knock, build a door."

—MILTON BERLE

In 2016, my arrangement with MyLifeLine continued to be flexible and part-time. This opened space for me to pursue a challenge I had been thinking about for years—starting my own consulting business.

Since college, I've always been passionate about organizational psychology and cultures that support people through personal and professional development. I thought I could take everything I'd learned through MyLifeLine to begin again on my own terms.

I called my new business Vital Biz Consulting and set to work designing a logo, website, and specific offerings, from business planning and hiring to teaching clients how to gain awareness of their communication styles and behavioral preferences. I've always been driven to learn what motivates people, and conversely, what stops them from growing or taking risks.

Just six months into my new consultancy, however, it was clear that MyLifeLine was in trouble. Fundraising was down under the leadership of another executive director. We had to dip into savings for the first time in our history. In addition, key staff members were stressed, burned out, and many weren't even speaking to each other.

The culture became so toxic that by the end of 2016, the MyLifeLine board asked the executive director to resign. During the holidays that year, I went through a period of internal reckoning. I had too much invested in the organization to see it fail. While I was excited to get my consultancy off the ground, it was obvious that this wasn't the right time. My exact thoughts were, "If MyLifeLine is going to fail, it's going to fail on my watch." MyLifeLine was my baby, and it needed emergency care.

With the Board's approval, I took back the reins as executive director of MyLifeLine in January 2017. In my office, there was a picture window looking out onto the gorgeous Rocky Mountains, a sight that always grounded me, even though I felt anything but calm and serene.

The MyLifeLine staff morale was in shreds, and things were far worse than I thought. Trust was broken, and there were significant wounds to heal across the organization. Amid this tense backdrop, my self-doubt kicked in regularly. *Who was I to think that I was qualified to turn around such a troubled organization?* Then again, my determination would push me forward . . . *Who better than me to do so? Trust yourself.*

As usual, I researched creative strategies and found *The First 90 Days* by Michael D. Watkins. This practical guide revealed a plan to help organizations in crisis. I followed the book's advice to the letter, and to my relief, the plan was working.

The first and most painful step was to cut costs drastically to restore financial health. This necessitated staff cuts and was the hardest thing I've ever had to do professionally. First to go was our administrative assistant, and then our operations director. These were people I knew well and really cared about.

In addition to laying off staff, I took a 33 percent cut in salary from the previous person in my position. I'm sure it helped staff to know that I was "walking the walk." After the layoffs, we streamlined operations with a lean staff of three people in addition to me: our fundraising director, program director, and IT developer.

My second priority was to fundraise to earn funds necessary to achieve our mission. We began planning for our May 2017 Derby fundraiser—also our ten-year anniversary. I personally contacted all our donors, volunteers, and sponsors throughout the years letting them know that I was back as executive director.

As important as it was to get MyLifeLine back on solid footing, I also wanted to accomplish two things: sustainability for the future and a bigger impact for cancer patients.

One question kept me up at night. What would it take for us to reach *every* cancer patient who needed a lifeline? When I read the book *Forces for Good: The Six Practices of High-Impact Nonprofits* by Heather McLeod Grant and Leslie R. Crutchfield, my thoughts gelled. I learned that for a nonprofit to maximize social impact, it must address three critical areas: direct services, policy, and research. MyLifeLine provided direct services, but not having research or policy arms put our long-term future at risk.

So, I began looking into how we could integrate research and policy initiatives. Everywhere I looked, two organizations came up repeatedly: American Cancer Society (ACS) and Cancer Support Community (CSC), both of whom we already had partnerships with, and both of whom had very successful research and policy programs. Suddenly the solution was crystal clear; we didn't need to reinvent the wheel. We needed to consider merging with another organization.

The Nonprofit Mergers Workbook: The Leader's Guide to Considering, Negotiating, and Executing a Merger by David La Piana became my bible. Among the things I learned is that the board would have to make the decision about the potential merger; my responsibility was to help influence and support the board in its decision-making process.

Next came an analysis to decide which of the two organizations was a better fit. While the American Cancer Society was our single largest referral source and a household name everyone knew, there was a lot of red tape and legal compliance issues to deal with. It had taken me four years just to cement our partnership with them. In addition, because the American Cancer Society was so huge, I worried that MyLifeLine would get swallowed up by them. I also didn't know their CEO or other key decision-makers.

On the other hand, the Cancer Support Community was the right size for us—a $10 million organization that was far leaner but still offered vital services for patients and caregivers. Some of the services included cancer support helplines, educational materials, and an affiliate network providing in-person support and health resources. They had also built The Research & Training Institute and the Cancer Policy Institute to study the psychosocial effects of a cancer diagnosis and advocate for systemic healthcare changes at the government level. These were the exact two "arms" that we needed to position MyLife-Line for growth. The only thing the Cancer Support Community was missing was the digital platform to build connection and community, which MyLifeLine offered.

To me, a merger with the Cancer Support Community was a no-brainer. I presented the idea to the Board, and while many were partial to the better-known American Cancer Society, they approved of me exploring a conversation with the Cancer Support Community. A week later, I was on a plane to meet with the organization's CEO, Kim Thiboldeaux, in Washington, DC. We had known each other for several years. In fact, she had mentioned the possibility of a merger years earlier to me, but it hadn't been the right time. Kim took me to lunch at a restaurant near their office, just two blocks from the White House, filled with people in power suits. Once seated and we had ordered from the menu, she took her glasses off and looked at me. Direct and to the point, she asked, "What's on your mind, Marcia?"

I dove in and began to paint the vision of a merger together. "As you know, we've been partnering with the Cancer Support Community for years. When I investigated creating research, policy, helpline, and educational offerings, I realized that your organization is already doing this work. But what the Cancer Support Community is missing is what we at MyLifeLine have been doing for ten years—providing cancer patients, caregivers, loved ones, and friends with a technology platform to enhance connection and communication. Our services are perfectly complementary, and there is no overlap. I'd like to open a discussion about a merger if you're interested."

Kim is extremely savvy and intelligent. Her response was reassuring. "Your timing is perfect. Our board has been talking about how to offer more digital services so that patients can access CSC from anywhere. MyLifeLine could fill this gap for us."

From there, our conversation was off and running. We talked for two hours about the possibilities and next steps. By the time I had to leave, Kim offered to run the idea past their Board. In an Uber on the way back to the airport, I called our board president, Jason Wagner, and told him how well the meeting had gone. We were elated.

In March 2017, our board meeting revolved around the topic of a potential merger. We formed a merger investigation committee. Both organizations signed confidentiality and nondisclosure agreements so we could begin exchanging sensitive information like financials, website metrics, and staff salaries.

Over the next few months, we worked on the merger analysis, due diligence process, and technology assessment. Our team organized years of records into a shared Dropbox folder with the Cancer Support Community.

That May, we celebrated MyLifeLine's tenth anniversary with our most successful fundraiser to date, raising nearly $300,000. Katrese and Chad Wheeler (our surrogate family) were honored with the George Karl *Courage Award*. Chad had unfortunately been diagnosed with esophageal cancer in May 2016—and their family used MyLifeLine to provide updates and connect with loved ones. This was a full-circle experience: Katrese had helped my family with infertility caused by cancer, and now we were supporting her family with their own devastating cancer journey.

Throughout that summer, Monique helped us produce a merger analysis report (she was also a founding board member of MyLifeLine). Both boards had one month to review the report, and all its information, before casting a vote to approve or decline the merger. During that process, I sought advice from a merger and acquisitions attorney to ensure we were complying with legal obligations.

In July, both boards voted to approve an "intent to merge," and a merger agreement was drafted. Next up was negotiating things like MyLifeLine staff being ensured jobs. The staff were guaranteed jobs if they wanted them. I assured them that the merger would help secure our future while also enabling us to serve many more patients and caregivers than we could have done otherwise.

That October, the merger was officially approved and would be effective on January 1, 2018. Losing autonomy over our independent organization was a gnawing concern, but the tremendous benefits to cancer patients strongly outweighed any trepidation I felt.

This was an incredibly busy time in my personal life as well. Jake and Ryan were twelve years old and in middle school, dealing with all the new challenges and demands that entailed.

On top of that, for the past few years, I had been suffering from lower back pain which became progressively debilitating. I could no longer sleep through the night. I had tried everything – chiropractor, acupuncture, spinal steroid shots, physical therapy, and medication – in the hopes of avoiding back surgery. Finally, I couldn't take the pain anymore. It felt like a knife stabbing into my lower back throughout the day and night. Finally, as a last resort, I searched for the best surgeon in Denver and scheduled the operation to fix my herniated disc and spinal stenosis.

November and December 2017 were intense and challenging. MyLifeLine was finalizing the merger agreement, and I was exhausted from the lack of sleep from back pain and anxiety over my impending surgery. I was also still negotiating staff salaries and roles, among all the other pieces to integrate. I finally signed the official merger agreement, but unfortunately, just at that time, my right-hand program director quit because she wanted a salary increase. I begged the new leadership to give her the $5K extra—she was more than worth it. I even offered to cut my salary by $5K to make it work. But they said no, which was upsetting, considering all we were doing to set ourselves up for success. I think it was short-sighted since hiring and training new people is far more costly than retaining current staff.

The day before the back surgery, my parents flew in to help me during recovery and lend a hand with the kids. Finally, the big day, December 8, arrived. I was casually handed a waiver, stating that I might die or be paralyzed on the operating table. Staring at the form, painful flashbacks came flooding back from my hysterectomy, when I didn't yet know I had cancer but was still forced to sign my organs away.

Luckily, the surgery went smoothly—and there were no surprises. The next seventy-two hours were extremely painful until the painkillers started working. One week later, I could stand and walk without feeling like a knife stabbing me in the back. The pain was gone! I felt incredibly grateful for another new lease on life.

In January 2018, three weeks after my surgery, the Cancer Support Community issued a press release announcing the merger as a big step forward for supporting cancer patients and families. My pride and excitement oozed into my work as I took on the newly created role of Vice President, Digital Strategy & Business Development. I would now be working with the smartest team of patient advocates at the Cancer Support Community and felt immense satisfaction at knowing we had turned our future around. Truly, I couldn't believe that I had gotten through the previous year in one piece. It had begun with despair and fear, and now the New Year was starting with abundant hope for a bright future.

16

STRONGER TOGETHER

"May your choices reflect your hopes, not your fears."

—NELSON MANDELA

For the first few months at the Cancer Support Community, we focused on integrating teams, platforms, processes, and systems. Being part of a growing team of patient advocates was very motivating. MyLife-Line was now able to incorporate opportunities to support research, policy, in-person support, education, a cancer helpline, and more. The merger was successful in leveraging synergies that better served cancer patients and families. Our digital footprint was expanded across the Cancer Support Community's 175 partner network and hospital systems. We streamlined administration and operations, so that funds could directly benefit our program and mission.

We were also gaining recognition from our peers, meaning our work was going in the right direction. The Cancer Support Community received the 2019 eHealthcare Leadership Award for Best Interactive Website as well as the 2020 Digital Media Health Award for best overall digital healthcare platform. All of the credit belongs to our hard-working digital operations team of rockstars; Jeff Coe, Jeanne Horne, Jenny Kim, Kathy Lindner, and Michael Rusho.

The Cancer Support Community was already a patient advocacy powerhouse in our field. The organization was a result of successfully merging two non-profit organizations, The Wellness Community and Gilda's Club, in 2009. Headquartered in Washington DC, the Cancer Support Community took a more active role in advocacy and policy changes on behalf of cancer patients. When the Obama administration created the Cancer Moonshot Initiative, led by Vice President Joe Biden, the Cancer Support Community joined a coalition to put patient needs at the center of our government's efforts. The goal was to accelerate cancer research to find a cure as soon as possible. The Moonshot channeled more than $1 billion into 240 research projects and 70 cancer science efforts. When President Obama left office, the Moonshot Initiative spun out of the government, and in 2017, Biden continued the momentum through the Biden Cancer Initiative. The Cancer Support Community participated on the board of the Biden Cancer Initiative and orchestrated a partnership with coalition partner, Airbnb, to provide free housing to cancer patients needing to travel for treatment.

When we were in merger negotiation talks, I was invited to the Cancer Support Community's 2017 Spring Gala in New York City. Then-Vice President Biden was the featured speaker and spoke urgently for forty minutes about his vision to end cancer quickly. Many know that Joe Biden lost his son Beau in 2015 to brain cancer. It was this trauma and grief that sparked his passion for helping other families. I was deeply moved by his personal story and genuine commitment to our shared mission.

Our team spearheaded exciting initiatives in my new role at the Cancer Support Community, including Colorado's Cancer Caregiver

Day, which was recognized at the Colorado State Capitol in Denver in 2018 with another proclamation signed by then-Governor John Hickenlooper, now a U.S. Senator.

The Cancer Support Community has long been committed to health equity for underrepresented populations. Upon learning that there were no cancer services or oncology treatments available on American Indian reservations, CSC built the first-ever cancer support center on an Indian reservation for the Navajo Nation in Arizona.

· · ·

Amidst the whirlwind of activity that marked my early months at the Cancer Support Community, I noticed how different the culture was from the one at MyLifeLine. I missed having the full authority to make people and culture decisions, so I volunteered to join the "True North" committee, organized by the human resources team. Together, with input from the entire forty-person staff, the True North committee developed an internal value system—guideposts for the organization's cultural expectations. In 2019, I was recognized with a "Chief Happiness Officer" award "for always coming into work with a smile." I really enjoyed my purpose there and tried to brighten people's days by finding ways to ensure that everyone felt valued.

My involvement with the True North committee revealed a rising passion in how work cultures impact business outcomes. Over my career, I have worked in a variety of cultures ranging from toxic to healthy. I learned early on that when a culture is healthy, employees are more engaged and productive. Research shows that when people are highly connected and committed to a company, then businesses are more successful. When employees feel appreciated, they stay longer and work harder—a win-win for all.

In my free time, I would study what the best cultures do and what motivates people. One of my favorite books on this topic is Drive: *The Surprising Truth About What Motivates Us* by Daniel H. Pink. The research is clear that human motivation is largely intrinsic, and that the aspects of this motivation can be divided into autonomy, mastery, and purpose. Armed with this knowledge, I would empower my teams with autonomy over their work lives, help them master new skills, and connect their work to their purpose.

17

PEOPLE MATTER MOST

*"How can we create a cultural legacy of happiness?
Let other people matter."*

—CHRISTOPHER PETERSON

On January 1, 2020, I wrote down my new year's resolution, which was to "create space." The pace of my life became so fast that I could no longer sustain it. Overwhelmed, I had no idea how to slow down. The boys were in eighth grade, and their lives were busier than ever. Between single parenting and a full-time career requiring frequent travel, I was running out of steam. You know . . . the quintessential hamster wheel that you can't get off.

And then came March 2020 when life as we knew it came to an abrupt halt. Travel ended. School ended. Sports ended. Activities ended. Yet suddenly, out of nowhere, I had *more space*. My space to stop, slow down, and rest. My new year's resolution had come true in the most unexpected way. With nowhere to go on weekends, I could finally slow down (and finish a puzzle or two—which was all the rage).

But COVID hit hard, especially those with cancer, and the Cancer Support Community didn't miss a beat. We quickly transitioned to remote working and established a COVID emergency fund for patients. I supported fundraising efforts to provide financial assistance to members of our community.

Because of the pandemic, our partner locations closed their doors, further eliminating access to vital services. Work became busy in new ways. We accelerated the design and development of new virtual programming. By July 2020, we produced online yoga classes and guided meditation videos specifically geared to those going through cancer treatment.

A major project in motion before the pandemic, our digital team launched a new website at CancerSupportCommunity.org to provide personalized guidance and information on specific cancer types with targeted resources. In addition, a new animated Virtual Patient Navigator named "Ruby" was created to deliver information about difficult health topics for people with no familiarity of cancer jargon.

• • •

The ongoing stress of the pandemic and challenges of navigating remote learning for the boys along with ever-increasing work responsibilities finally caught up with me by the summer of 2020. I needed to take a real break. Work-life boundaries had blurred for all of us. Working from home during a pandemic was a distinct privilege I am grateful for. But the flip side was we didn't just work from home, we lived at work.

Like so many others, I couldn't help but wonder, *Is this what I want in life?*

While COVID stay-at-home orders dragged on, and the death toll rose, I took a much-needed vacation with my boys. Not much was open, so we took a road trip. As we drove on long stretches of open roads from Colorado to Wyoming to Utah, I thought about how quickly time seemed to be moving. Life was spinning out of control. High school was fast approaching, and we had no idea what to expect with school reopenings. There were no vaccines available yet, so everyone was anxious amid all the uncertainty. If a global pandemic didn't inspire me to reflect on life choices, then I don't know what would.

I'd been with the Cancer Support Community for two-and-a-half years, and MyLifeLine was on solid ground. For me personally though, the urge to move on was impossible to ignore. Apart from feeling tapped out, I needed to pay attention to the physical symptoms I'd begun to experience—insomnia, low energy, and stomach pains. I meditated, prayed, and wrote in my journal until I recognized it was time for me to let go of MyLifeLine. Once again, I had to make room for someone else to take it to the next level.

But what next? My friend Angela bought me the book *Designing Your Life* by Bill Burnett and Dave Evans. It guided me to begin tracking the daily tasks that both energized and drained me. What became obvious was that I was drained from the constant hustle of fundraising and applying for grants. I was energized when connecting patients and caregivers with resources, fostering meaningful staff and volunteer connections, and speaking passionately about the Cancer Support Community's mission to diverse audiences. It also brought me joy to brighten someone's day by offering encouragement and appreciation.

What I yearned for was a creative way to help others achieve health, happiness, and personal and professional growth. Going back to my roots—my interest in human resources and organizational psychology in college—started to feel like my next professional calling.

After much deliberation, I decided to resign from the Cancer Support Community in September 2020, giving four weeks' notice. For the rest of 2020, I gave myself space to figure out my next steps.

Trust yourself. Leap, and a net will appear.

What I found especially helpful was an online coaching program called the PAVE Challenge, created by Nina Cashman. In this program, I gave myself permission to reflect on my next career move. Nina labeled this point between jobs as a "transitional hallway." Since I had been going at full speed for so long, I was excited to step off the tread-mill for a short while to choose my next move with intention.

Now that remote work options were booming after COVID, I saw opportunities everywhere. With over a decade of non-profit leader-ship, organizational culture, and business development experience, my intuition was nudging me to take a risk and evolve my career path. My plan was not to jump into the next first job but to wait for the *right* job.

I began by checking Indeed and LinkedIn. I treated my "transi-tional hallway" experiment as a business research project. My mission was to find work that excited me and allowed me to serve others by using my strengths in strategic thinking, building relationships, and bringing new ideas to the table. To this end, I conducted dozens of informal informational interviews with connections made over the last twenty years of my work life. I refreshed my LinkedIn profile and was relentless about perusing job ads. I quickly learned that if you send a resume to a company through a website, it drops into a black hole. It's so true that who you know matters, and that's how I found my next role.

In December 2020, a friend referred me to a potential consulting job with the Colorado Education Initiative, helping them monetize their digital community. While it wasn't my dream assignment because it involved fundraising, I loved their mission and was excited to share my expertise with another nonprofit organization.

Landing a months-long consulting project gave me the reason I needed to resuscitate Vital Biz, my previous consulting practice. Truth be told, I didn't like sending in resumes to black holes and the feeling of having to wait for someone else to call me. I'd rather control my destiny. I had been creating my own jobs for years; there was no reason I couldn't successfully do so again. Just like that, I breathed new life into Vital Biz Consulting, and soon more opportunities came knocking.

• • •

Three months after resigning from the Cancer Support Community, I sat on the floor with a new spiral-bound journal. It was New Year's Day 2021, the perfect time to listen within and imagine my "what next." My pen moved across the page in my first entry of the year: "My dream job would be titled Chief Culture Officer."

After deep reflection and the encouragement of coaches Nina Cashman, Gayle Lantz, and JC Heinen, I was inspired to focus on the health of employees, staff, and organizational cultures as a strategy to achieve financial growth and innovation.

How to land a chief culture officer role evaded me, but I made it my job to master new skill sets and expertise so that I would be ready when the opportunity presented itself. I studied servant leadership, cultural frameworks, and change management. I took courses to modernize my skills, including a course in Zoom virtual event production and Miro virtual collaboration tools. I got certified as a Professional Agile Coach and in leadership frameworks focused on purpose and people. Through TTI Success Insights, I earned multiple certifications in the Prioritized Leader Suite and became a driving forces analyst and behavioral analyst to help people understand their strengths, motivators, communication styles, and behavioral preferences.

That March, I began consulting with Rx4Good, a boutique patient advocacy firm that works with biopharma companies and healthcare organizations. I already knew and respected the people at this agency and fell in love with their culture led by CEO Ann Moravick.

But just as I was onboarding new assignments for Rx4good, I got a phone call that completely changed my trajectory. Ken Scalet, a long-time board member of the Cancer Support Community who had helped put our merger together, informed me that the CEO had unexpectedly quit. "Would you consider submitting your name for CEO?" he asked.

In shock, I mustered up the presence of mind to tell him I needed time to think. It had only been six months since my departure. As I stared out the window onto the vastness of the Rocky Mountain range, I couldn't help but notice the parallels to what had happened a few years earlier. Just as I began to generate business with Vital Biz, my "baby" (MyLifeLine/the Cancer Support Community) came calling. Part of me wondered if I'd ever be able to get Vital Biz up and running.

For a few days, I considered the possibilities until the answer became clear. I expressed to Ken that I did not wish to pursue the CEO role. It would have meant lots of fundraising, the activity I found most draining. However, I would be honored to support the organization in another meaningful way. The people and culture were in need of some tender loving care as it pertained to increasing staff burnout caused by the pandemic, leadership turnover, and the challenges of creating connection within a newly distributed workforce. With new strategies in my toolbelt, a deep knowledge of the Cancer Support Community's culture and staff, and a genuine affinity for the people and mission, I could make a difference.

I asked Ken if he would consider creating the role of Chief Culture Officer. Without hesitation, he said "Yes, let's make it happen. How soon can you start?"

And just like that, the vision I had for myself, made only four months earlier, came into being. If you don't think manifestations work, I am living proof that they do. As television personality and author Steve Harvey said, "You have not, because you ask not. You must write it down."

The Chief Culture Officer position was structured as a consulting arrangement through Vital Biz. This way, I wouldn't have to let Vital Biz go, and the Cancer Support Community did not have to commit to this role permanently. We determined that I would fulfill this role until they hired their next CEO.

Life is full of surprising turns, and today I know that so much is beyond my—or anyone's—control. What matters is being able to look back and recognize the lessons you've learned and relationships you've created along the way. Resilience, determination, and sheer grit are necessary ingredients in this bumpy road called life. Give yourself some credit, and *celebrate* your accomplishments, big and small.

When CSC hired their new CEO after almost a year of searching, I transferred my responsibilities to her.

Now I am working on a culture leadership book and training to help other non-profit organizations and corporations in the health sector design and implement their own culture for our post-pandemic world. At CSC, I piloted a new culture framework that identifies five pillars for culture success based on decades of research–it's called the CARES™ strategy: an acronym for Commitment, Appreciation, Respect, Engagement, and Safety. Because the model was successful in driving up engagement and psychological safety, I will continue building on this framework to help other organizations.

As David Brooks writes in his book *The Second Mountain*, "prioritize your loves." This allows us to prioritize what's most important according to our own unique values and purpose. Staying centered with a practice of gratitude, and an attitude of service, has been key to turning setbacks into stepping stones.

When we prioritize our loves, we prioritize our lives.

LOVE AT LAST

"I'm looking for love. Real love, ridiculous, inconvenient, consuming, can't-live-without-each-other love."

—CARRIE BRADSHAW, SEX IN THE CITY

Five years after my divorce, a rare and serendipitous thing happened. I met someone on the night of our 2019 Kentucky Derby fundraiser. After years of online dating and a couple of short-lived boyfriends, I certainly wasn't expecting to meet the love of my life.

Our Derby event took place at the Four Seasons in downtown Denver and brought together hundreds of supporters, donors, sponsors, volunteers, friends, and members of MyLifeLine. The event—like all Kentucky Derby viewing parties—is a parade of women dressed in pastel dresses, strappy heels, and signature big-brimmed Derby hats, and men in bowties, sear-sucker suits, and shirts and socks in every color of the rainbow. It's a festive, happy occasion that combines the spectacle of the race itself followed by a ceremony to honor cancer survivors and families who have been part of our MyLife-Line community.

When our event ended, I made my way to the public after-party in the main lobby of the hotel. That year we raised roughly $300,000, the highest yet; I felt both proud and confident as I joined the bar scene in my pink and gray flowered dress and silver fascinator. I was looking for my friend Angela, but my eyes diverted to the handsome stranger wearing a white and navy polka-dotted shirt and yellow bow tie suddenly standing in front of me.

"Hi, I'm Jim," he said, extending his hand. "What's your name?"

The band was crazy loud as people around us were dancing wild and drunk on mint juleps. Still, it was hard not to notice Jim's warm hazel eyes and cute dimples.

"My name is Marcia. I'm looking for Angela! Come find me later!" I dashed off in search of my friend.

Some twenty minutes later, I sat with Angela and several other friends who had been at the Cancer Support Community fundraiser. Out of the corner of my eye, I saw Jim walking toward me. My heart skipped a beat.

"Hi Angela!" He smiled widely with mock emphasis.

"No, I'm *Marcia* . . . my *friend* is Angela."

I giggled at his misunderstanding of my intro earlier. He apologized, we had a good laugh, and the next thing we knew, friends dragged us onto the dance floor when the DJ played "Sweet Child of Mine" by Guns N' Roses. Before the night ended, Jim asked for my number as we planned to meet for dinner that week.

One date turned into several, and I liked him more each time.

Over the next few months, I noticed Jim had a kindness and ease about him that was charming and endearing. He was comfortable in his own skin, but there was something more, too. There was a sensitivity about him that radiated. I soon understood why. Jim was not only a quality assurance engineer in the FinTech industry, but he was also a professional artist showing in galleries around the country. Here's a guy who ran complicated software test automation for banks by day, and then spent his weekends painting expressionist realism art. Art connoisseurs regularly buy and commission him for New York cityscapes and bar scenes shadowed in dark, misty tones. Jim told me he thrives when using both the left and right sides of his brain. It didn't hurt that his sense of humor was perfect for me, and he has been thoughtful in a million little and big romantic ways. On many occasions, he would surprise me with a favorite gift, a bouquet of yellow sunflowers, or a specific jewel-toned necklace I had admired in a store once.

Is it any wonder I fell hard? Love is a mystery, but that night the stars were aligned. Jim and I have been inseparable ever since, and I couldn't be more excited to see what the future holds.

EPILOGUE

"In this world, there is no force equal to the strength of a woman determined to rise."

—W.E.B. DU BOIS, AMERICAN SOCIOLOGIST, HISTORIAN, AUTHOR, AND ACTIVIST

How rewarding it feels to live a life that feels genuine on so many levels. My own experiences revealed how unpredictable life is and how seldom we get to anticipate the curveballs. Planning is paramount to success, yet we must be willing to reframe plans should something else be required of us. I still struggle with stress and overwhelm just like everyone else. But in the deepest possible sense, I trust in my capacity to be resilient when challenges block my way.

My boys are now teenagers figuring out who they are while paving the way to pursue their own bold dreams. Motherhood at this stage is a delicate balance of letting go and holding on. My goal is to love them unconditionally and nurture their independence while also guiding their development with a steady hand. I am very proud of all that my sons have overcome and confident they are each building the strength of character and emotional grit necessary for life success.

Here's a bit of coaching wisdom I regularly practice. The next time life throws a boulder or two your way, try this simple formula: Pause. Pivot. Propel.

1. **Pause:** When things feel chaotic, it's better to stop and respond than to react from a place of fatigue and overwhelm. Give yourself time and space to reflect on what's happening and what's most important to focus on right now. Meditation and journaling are two practices that have worked wonders for me to gain clarity and perspective. When I use these tools each morning, I view challenges in a healthier way.

2. **Pivot:** Rigid thinking keeps us stuck and unable to see beyond our own narrow lens. The question to ask is, "What's possible now?" There's so much optimism in those three magic words! When we pivot our thoughts to recognize all that is possible, the path before us widens. Suddenly, we're open to new ways of seeing and being in the world. Pivoting is what allows us to bend—not break—with the wind.

3. **Propel:** If pivoting allows you to look at your life through a broader lens, this stage is all about taking the necessary action steps to move forward. When you notice things start to "click" and make sense, you will feel the "propel" happen. Ride it! And keep going in the direction of your dreams.

I view the Pause-Pivot-Propel model as a kind of North Star. It's what keeps me agile, adaptable, and imbued with a growth mindset—all of which are key leadership skills necessary for the Roaring 2020s and beyond. Time and again, I've seen how this framework helps turn setbacks into stepping stones, while also honoring the ways life mysteriously unfolds.

The only real constant in life is personal choice. For my part, if I stay in learning mode, then I can improve and fulfill my purpose that has been crystal clear to me since I first started working decades ago—to truly connect with and help others. When I follow that thread, I'm on the right track. What is the most important thread in your life that brings you joy and fulfillment?

I continue to be guided by personal values like integrity, respect, and optimism. Today, I am clear that the people I choose to share my life with need to share those values, too. People talk about post-traumatic growth, and I very much believe in it. Learning from setbacks is the only way to bring about positive change and growth.

When COVID hit, I pushed the career pause button and pivoted toward building empowering, inclusive work cultures that maximize the potential of all employees. Striking out on my own in 2020, I launched a culture coaching, training, and consulting practice. Today, I work as a fractional (contract) Chief Culture Officer for healthcare companies ready to leverage the power of culture to earn *Great Place to Work for All* awards.

This new business venture is a continuation of my mission to help leaders and employees advocate for themselves in the work setting. I can already imagine the dozens if not hundreds of business case studies that this era of post-COVID will inspire. We are in uncharted territory—all of us trying to figure out how to work, how to live, and how to maintain our balance when everything feels off-kilter. Regarding connection, that all-important water cooler talk isn't going to happen as much in the future, so how do we foster relationships, trust, and collaboration in different ways?

We are all connected, even though it might not feel like it sometimes. I have seen the power of community that MyLifeLine fosters amongst its members. I have felt it through the various upheavals in my life. And I know that authentic connection will get us through the current day and all the days to come.

My wish for you is threefold: that you pause to honor your key connections, that you have the courage to pivot when change is needed, and that growth propels you forward, turning every setback into a new stepping stone.

You are meant for great things.

ACKNOWLEDGEMENTS

To my parents, Ken and Nancy Levin —for your unwavering support up the mountains and down the valleys of life. By raising me on a strong foundation of Jewish values, including generosity and compassion, you set me up for success through your unconditional love. You inspire me to be the best version of myself. I am sorry for the trouble I caused you as a teenager.

To Meryl Gion—you are my favorite sister and best friend, the one who gets me and understands the crazy language we made up together as kids. I could never have walked this road without you. You have smoothed the hard edges of life's toughest moments. Peter, thank you for being a caring brother-in-law to me and uncle to Jake and Ryan. We all love you.

To Katrese Wheeler—for your pivotal role in my life. You are my "soul sister." Without you stepping up to be our surrogate mom, I would not have experienced motherhood. From the day I met you and your amazing husband Chad, my world opened to the possibilities of becoming a mom. Thank you from the bottom of my heart for your grace, grit, strength, and enduring friendship.

To Rob Donziger—I couldn't have asked for a better partner with whom to co-parent. Not only have you made the journey of parenthood possible, but you also give our boys all they need from a father—unconditional love, support, and guidance. Thank you.

To Nancy Sharp and Sarah Zimmerman—my Dream Team. I appreciate your powerful guidance in weaving my life stories into this book. Nancy, if it weren't for your Guided Autobiography classes in 2020, this spark of an idea would not have come to fruition. You helped me sift meaning and purpose out of the darkest times. I've enjoyed sharing this creative journey with you. Thank you for making the book creation process both fun and educational.

To Angela Hartshorn—thank you for reading this manuscript with discerning eyes and providing wise feedback to help the story flow. You always cheer me on in my wildest adventures, and I appreciate your friendship so much.

To Jim Beckner—Your love is exactly what I've prayed for all these years. Most of all, thank you for making me laugh every day and helping me see new, artistic perspectives. To Hadley and Sophie, I love you both and am lucky to witness you grow and blossom. You make everything better and brighter.

To my beautiful childhood, college, flight attendant, and life-long friends—you each bring a unique joy to my life, and I know we always have each other's backs— Bonnie Besade, Shani Boone, Lisa Burns, Ginger Fairchild, Kim Franz, Chrissi Gelson, Sara Hungerford, Jeannine Jacobi, Vicki Larson, Nickie Lee, Linda Miller, Cindy "Belly Dancer" Morrison, Wendra Reese, Carrin Reid, Sharon Ronen, Kate Szymanski, and Sue Toomey. A special note of gratitude goes to Annie Shugarman who flew across the country to take care of me at Northwestern Memorial hospital in Chicago during my sickest days.

To the founding board members of MyLifeLine—you have a special place in my heart. You took a chance to transform the cancer experience through community and connection. You pioneered the idea to build an online cancer community and gave generously of your time and resources with the mission to serve hundreds of thousands of people impacted by cancer. Thank you for making it happen— Monique Brenno, Rob Donziger, Alison and Kent Muckel, Dr. Lisa Schatz, Katrese Wheeler, and Cari Wolff.

To the key staff, supporters, and volunteers who built MyLife-Line over ten years---your hard work and contributions are truly appreciated. In alphabetical order: Nicole Baillis, Melissa Bowen, Christi Cahill, Jeff Coe, Dr. Rob Fisher, Jeanne Horne, Kimberly Irvine, Pam Jones, Coach George Karl, Jan Kolodny, Kathy Lindner, Richard Male, Chef Shayna Martin, Tricia McEuen, Margo McInturf, Jen Mills, Jill Mitchell, Laurel Montag, Rabbi Anat Moskowitz, David Oine, Kristin Olson, Michael Rusho, Adrienne Schaffer, Jen Thomas, Janie Trevor, Kim Van Deraa, Dennis Wakabayashi, Maria Watson, and Adam Wright.

A special shout-out the final team of MyLifeLine Board Members—you played a vital role in the merger with Cancer Support Community. You helped see our vision all the way through. In alphabetical order: Roberta Aberle (in loving memory), Gregg Denhoffer, Allen Dodge, Barb Findley, Bob Graham, Dave Hicks, Laurie Hicks, Jack Hill, Lizzy Morton, David Oine, Matt Rawley, Susan Rawley, Greg Schowe, and our fearless Board President, Jason Wagner.

To the Cancer Support Community (CSC) leadership team— my gratitude goes out to Linda Bohannon, Jill Durovsik, Ken Scalet, Kim Thiboldeaux, and Jeff Travers for believing that our organizations would create a bigger impact together. You warmly welcomed and successfully integrated MyLifeLine into CSC and continue to champion the MyLifeLine online community ensuring that no one faces cancer alone.

In loving memory of friends and loved ones gone from this earth
. . . and never forgotten:

Roberta Aberle

Jax Arcaris

Lori Aquila Anderson

Matt Fairchild

Ruben Garza

Kelley Gleason

Monica Knoll

Darlene Mader

Ivy Pregozen

Rochelle Shoretz

Leslie Sinclair

Shane Snyder

Chad Wheeler

My paternal grandparents, Leo and Ellie Levin

My maternal grandparents, Nathan and Molly Prager

And finally, to Tami Borrego—my college best friend and room-
mate who instilled a seed long ago that I was meant for great things.
What a gift. Your kindness was a stepping stone that powered me
through many setbacks for decades to come.

And to my readers, if you made it this far, thank you. You never
know how deeply your words may resonate with others needing to hear
them. Stating that you truly believe in a friend or family member *may
shape that person's future belief* in themselves. Tell a child, or someone
else you love, that they are meant for GREAT THINGS, and just as
important, *say it to yourself.* Repeatedly. Because it's true.

AUTHOR'S NOTE

This memoir was written from memories excavated from my 50+ year old brain, personal journals, documents, photos, and records kept over the years. To protect the identities of certain individuals, details and names of the following were modified: Danny and Ed.

ABOUT THE AUTHOR

MARCIA DONZIGER is a fractional Chief Culture Officer supporting mission-driven organizations to level up their impact and influence by leading with confidence, clarity, and courage. She is the architect of the Culture CARES™ Strategic Framework, built to help today's organizations thrive.

In 2007, Marcia founded the national nonprofit organization, MyLifeLine Cancer Foundation, with a vision to transform the cancer experience through community and connection. She served in various leaderships roles for more than a decade and led the successful merger of the organization into the Cancer Support Community in 2018.

Marcia holds a degree in Organizational Psychology and Business Management, is a certified Agile Coaching Professional, and regularly presents to national and international audiences about workplace culture and engagement. Marcia lives in Denver, Colorado, with her twin boys and feels enormously grateful to have lived cancer-free since 1997.

To inquire about speaking, coaching, or consulting, please visit www.MarciaDonziger.com.